THE BEST BAGELS
ARE MADE AT HOME

Dona Z. Meilach

BRISTOL PUBLISHING ENTERPRISES
San Leandro, California

A Nitty Gritty® Cookbook

Printed in the United States of America.

ISBN 1-55867-131-5

Cover design: Frank Paredes
Cover photography: John Benson
Food stylist: Suzanne Carreiro

CONTENTS

ACKNOWLEDGMENTS

Many thanks go to my Scrabble® opponent, Ellis Willson, whose gift of a bread machine turned me on to its wonders and propelled me headlong into the bagel adventure.

Special gratitude to: John Marx, Marx Hot Bagel Factory, Inc., Cincinnati, OH; Ben Lang, The Bagel Boyz, Encinitas, CA; Baltimore Bagels, Encinitas, CA; and all the anonymous bagel bakeries I visited whose personnel shared their menus and processes with me.

Finally, I am indebted to the testers, tasters and readers whose experiences and comments helped tremendously: Sue Kaye, Patrick Worley, Vern Wright, Madeline and Syd Goode, Fern and Ralph Ritchie, Susan and Richard Seligman. And of course, a bagel-shaped medal goes to my husband, Dr. Mel Meilach, whose criticisms and encouragements are always provided with humor, patience and wonderment.

Dona Meilach
Carlsbad, California

ALL ABOUT BAGELS

Bagels — warm, fresh, comforting, satisfying and wonderful tasting. Overflowing baskets of bagels are showing up in incredible bagel shops, in supermarket bread bins, delis, frozen food counters, even on vendors' push carts in shopping malls and on street corners throughout the country. People are standing in lines to buy them by the dozen for breakfast, a mid-morning nosh, luncheon sandwiches and bagel brunches. They're replacing the venerable sweet roll for office breaks because they're appealing, appetizing, tasty, and low in calories and fat.

Since 1994, bagels have shown a 37% increase in popularity, according to surveys reported in bakery trade magazines. That consumption is expected to increase by 30% or more each year. Bagel bakeries, even in moderate-sized cities, sell upwards of 300 dozen bagels on weekdays and 700 dozen on weekends. In addition to the proliferating number of bagel shops and local and national bagel chains, doughnut and hamburger chains are selling bagels. They're served routinely on the luxury cruise liner, the QE2. In a television advertisement, a national jelly-making company shows bagels as the ideal vehicle for its luscious jellies and jams. An ad in a computer magazine announces that bagels and cream cheese will be served at a board of director's meeting — implying that bagels will entice people to attend.

WHAT IS A BAGEL?

A bagel is traditionally a hefty, dense ring of somewhat bland-tasting bread. But with different flours, such as rye and wheat, bagels take on different tastes. Add raisins, blueberries, strawberries, dates and nuts for a dessert-like bagel. Add veggies, onions, poppy seeds, peanut butter and other ingredients for an infinite variety of taste combinations.

The popularity of bagels is as much attributed to what you can put on them and in them as to what you add to the unbaked dough. They are the perfect vehicles for spreads. Most often spreads consist of a cream cheese base that may be mixed with salmon or lox, fruits, vegetables and spices — in myriad combinations. There are regional differences in how bagels are made, and ongoing arguments about what constitutes the "perfect" bagel and best spread combination.

The traditional bagel sandwich consists of cream cheese, lox, a slice of onion and a slice of tomato. But that's only the beginning. Bagel sandwiches are so popular that bagel bakeries often list 40 or 50 sandwich variations on their menus. Then there are mini bagels and bialys. For catered bagel brunches, there are 3- to 6-pound bagels that are filled and then cut into pie-shaped wedges.

Bagels have a lot going for them. They don't crush or smash while being carried; they don't melt from the heat or suffer from freezing. They're at their optimum goodness when fresh and hot out of the oven, but they're delicious, too, even when frozen, thawed and toasted. If they get stale, they can be made into bagel chips or ground into breadcrumbs. They're an all-around convenient, no-waste food product that is well suited to today's health-conscious consumers.

The plain water bagel is low in calories compared to other traditional breakfast foods. Estimates as to the number of calories in a bagel differ, and its size is a factor. Most bagels average 4 to 5 ounces, and tally up to between 150 to 200 calories. The addition of nuts, raisins, berries, chocolate chips and other ingredients will add to the count. I saw a cracked wheat bagel in a health food store that had 320 calories. Some bagels weigh 6 ounces. Mini bagels may be 1 to 3 ounces, so the calories vary accordingly.

It's the toppings and spreads that shoot up the calorie tab, though this can be tempered by using light and fat-free cheeses, and spreads without cheese. A whopping dollop of cream cheese slapped onto each half of a bagel (2 tablespoons of cream cheese have 10 grams of fat and 100 calories) will wipe out the innocence of the plain bagel. Two tablespoons of regular preserves (there are sugar-free varieties, too) can add on 50 calories but no fat. And peanut butter? Well, you would rather not know, if you're counting calories and grams of fat.

Still, you're better off with bagels than with a doughnut, which has 176 calories and 11 grams of fat. A homemade bran muffin (not the giant restaurant or bakery size) has 112 calories and 5 grams of fat. A large croissant has 300 calories, 17 grams of fat and 85 milligrams of cholesterol. The butter will do it every time. There is no butter in a bagel recipe. Only egg bagels have cholesterol; even that can be eliminated by using egg whites instead of a whole egg (or ¼ cup liquid egg substitute). But a sweet roll with nut and raisin Danish filling, and icing, can top them all with about 360 calories, 22.3 grams of fat and 82.2 milligrams of cholesterol.

WHERE DID BAGELS COME FROM? A LITTLE HISTORY...

There doesn't seem to be one dominant story about the origin of bagels, though a common thread weaves through them all. In her book, *Jewish Cooking in America*, Joan Nathan says, "The boiled and baked roll with a hole dates possibly from the Roman period."

However, the bagel in America apparently is a descendant of Polish ancestors. It dates to 1863 when the Polish general, John Sobieski, rescued Vienna from the Turks. When Sobieski returned from his victorious battle and rode his horse through the town, the grateful populace clung to the stirrups of his saddle, which were called "breugels." In honor of this triumphant deed, they fashioned bread in the shape of his stirrups and called it by that name. Eventually, the stirrup shape became round and the name became "bagel." (Some historians think the French croissant shape also attributes its origin to the replica of a stirrup.)

Another story is that the word derives from the German word, "beigen," which means "to bend," and that the bagel is a descendant of the pretzel. Still another story is that the bagel's round hole developed so that street vendors in Poland and Russia could pile the bread on poles and carry them around more easily to sell from their carts.

The American Bagel

Bagels found their way to America via the Polish immigration of the late 1800's, but were popular only among the Polish Jews who settled in New York. Between 1910 and 1915 a Bagel Bakers' Local #338 union formed. Eventually, men who apprenticed to the first 300 bakers of that union moved to different parts of the country. In the early 1950's, the Broadway comedy, *Bagels and Yox*, played to standing-room-only audiences, and bagels were distributed during intermission. Soon after, *Time* and *Family Circle* magazines ran recipes for "bageles."

Harry Lender, who had emigrated from Lublin, Poland, taking his cue from the interest generated by the magazine articles, converted his New Haven, Connecticut, bakery into a bagel bakery. In 1955, Lender and his son, Murray, packaged their bagels to sell to supermarkets. In 1960, the first bagel-making machine, invented by Dan Thompson, was introduced. All bagels had been made by hand before then. By 1962, the Lenders began freezing bagels and marketing them nationally.

Bagels began a known, traceable thread in their westward emigration in 1967.

Eddie Kaye and Harold Block, who had been sent to the Midwest by their New York garment industry companies, and their wives, bemoaned their inability to buy bagels in this "hinterland outpost." In an interview, Kaye's wife, Sue, now living in Carlsbad, California, told me they contacted a New York friend whose father was an old-time bagel baker, and used his recipes to open their first bakery in Columbus, Ohio, called Hot Bagels, Inc. Following its success, they opened another in Cincinnati and hired John Marx, a former bouncer in a Cincinnati bar, as a manager.

Eventually Marx bought the bakeries, sponsored sports teams and athletic events, advertised on TV and on the teams' tee shirts, and his bagel bakery boomed. Marx, who is neither Polish nor Jewish, currently operates three very successful Cincinnati bagel bakeries called Marx Hot Bagels Factory, Inc., d/b/a Marx Hot Bagels. Occasionally, John wears his Bagelman outfit, which he first designed in 1971, when he was invited to demonstrate how to hand-roll bagels for a folk festival at the Smithsonian Museum in Washington, D.C. Then CBS's Charles Kuralt spent an entire day filming an "On the Road" sequence at Marx's tiny, but very busy, bakery. Marx now makes bagels in about 50 varieties. He also spends a lot of time in his red Bagelman cap, shorts, cape and blue tights, speaking to schoolchildren about the importance of learning to read and staying in school.

With bagel bakeries opening everywhere today, their names are as varied as the flavors and assortment of spreads they offer. There are Baltimore Bagels, Garden State

Bagels, Top-O-The-Bagel, I-N-Joy Bagels and others. The Bagel Boyz, operated by brothers from South Africa, is a play on the words "bagel boys." In that country a "bagel boy" is a young man who is used to having everything and living in the lap of luxury. "As a child, my grandmother made bagels every Sunday morning," explained Ben Lang, owner of Bagel Boyz in Encinitas, California. "Her bagels were very hard and chewy and tasted completely different from those we bake in America."

Bagels have become a favored food in far corners of the world. I noshed on them at the Hong Kong Bagel Bar. I found a bagel bakery doing a booming business near the University of Texas in Austin. In the past couple of years, five bagel bakeries have opened within a few miles of my southern California home. In Peoria, Illinois, I bought huge, soft bagels in a giant discount food store. The expression, "If it plays in Peoria, it will play anywhere," apparently applies to bagels, too.

HOMEMADE BAGELS AND SPREADS

Inevitably the popularity of bagels is inspiring home bakers to flour their bread boards, heat up their ovens and bake bagels.

Bread machines have revolutionized home bread baking and removed the tedium of mixing and kneading dough. We've targeted bagel recipes that we've tested specifically for bread machines —a foolproof process when ingredients are measured and timing followed. The same recipes are a breeze to make in a food processor, with a heavy-duty electric mixer or by hand. We also describe how dough rises quickly in a microwave oven, thereby reducing the preparation and processing time considerably. Using the combination of food processor or electric mixer and microwave means you can literally have bagels from dough to oven in about 25 minutes.

Boiling is the important step that gives bagels their unmatched chewable quality and adds the distinctive shine to the crusty surface. It's a deceptively easy task. Boiling the shaped dough is like making pasta, but faster and easier. It's certainly easier than making croissants, for example.

You can make bagels of almost any flavor and size, given the parameters of your kneading ability, and the size of your boiling or "kettling" pot and oven. A 1½-pound bread machine recipe produces 8 to 12 bagels, depending on the size of the bagels. Hand-mixing and heavy-duty electric mixers can deal with larger dough batches.

Why Make Bagels At Home When They Are So Readily Available?

You can load them with your favorite ingredients and really taste them. I've tasted and analyzed many good commercially made bagels, but some have one or two raisins in a raisin-cinnamon bagel, one chip in a chocolate chip bagel and no taste at all in a pineapple-coconut bagel, with no sign of any pineapple. If I hadn't read the bin label, I would have thought I was eating a plain bagel.

The aroma of baking bagels will have your family tumbling out of bed in the morning, anxious to eat them warm right from the oven. Make them for guests — they'll talk about it for years.

The satisfaction of shaping dough and creating delicious bagels is hard to describe. Children revel in taking a ball of dough, working a few raisins or chocolate chips into it, and then punching a hole through it. They follow the process through boiling and baking until they see "their" bagel, shiny and hot, emerge from the oven.

Finally, your homemade bagels will have no preservatives and no artificial flavoring. When you bake bagels, you know what's going into them. And if you're allergic to any flours normally used, it's easy to find substitutes.

In this book, along with innovative recipes for bagels, you'll find suggestions for spreads, sandwiches and canapés. Use these for homemade bagels and also for bagels you buy. Most bagel stores and delis offer a dozen or so spreads and sandwiches, some inspired, but most are ordinary because they're the ones that sell the best. At home, you have triple the choice. Any will look elegant and taste *haute gourmet* if you serve them for bagel brunches, lunches and at different holidays. The cranberry spreads, for example, will delight your family and guests for Thanksgiving.

What is the real test of a good bagel? If you and your family like them, that's all that matters. Fortunately, there are no tests, no standards. No one can agree on what is "best." So surge forward. Bake bagels and embellish them according to your tastes.

TOOLS OF THE BAGEL BAKER'S TRADE

For **bread machine** bagel making, you will need measuring cups, measuring spoons, a rolling pin, plastic wrap, nonstick vegetable spray, a bread board, a 4- to 6-quart soup pot for boiling the bagels, a tea towel for draining them, a slotted spatula, a couple of baking sheets (preferably double aluminum or Teflon-coated) and a pastry brush. A bagel cutter is optional, depending on how you shape the bagels.

To make bagels by hand, with a heavy-duty mixer with a dough hook, or with a food processor, you'll need the equipment required for the bread machine preparation, plus bowls, rubber spatulas and mixing spoons. Bagel dough needs to be relatively stiff, and mechanical tools make quick work of an otherwise tedious process.

OTHER USEFUL EQUIPMENT

An **instant-reading oven or baker's thermometer** for checking water temperature is handy, but optional. A **food scale** is useful for weighing dough if you're trying to maintain a consistent size and weight for the bagels. A **ruler** for marking off lengths of dough or circle sizes on your kneading board will also help achieve consistent sizes.

Get a good **serrated knife** for cutting bagels easily. (Remember always to cut with the blade away from your fingers!) There are many special **bagel holders**. There are

Lucite and wooden holders with slits on both sides that allegedly wedge the bagel in so you don't have to hold it. The slits guide the knife blade through the middle. For example, the "Bagel Biter" is a plastic holder with a blade mounted within. Place the bagel in the holder, pull the handle over the base and push down so the blade cuts the bagel. The "Bagel Trap" holds the bagel tight with a spring arm so you can slice it into 2, 3 or 4 slices. There are also special **bagel toasters** with wider slots than a conventional toaster.

The easiest **baking pan** available to most home cooks is an aluminum cookie sheet or a flat nonstick Teflon-coated sheet pan. A **baking stone** made of unglazed tile and sold in housewares shops as a pizza stone provides dry, intense direct heat that helps give bagels a crisp crust. Ordinary unglazed quarry tiles sold in tile shops are an inexpensive substitute. Tiles should be slightly less than ½-inch thick; if they are too thick, they will take too long to heat up, and if they're too thin, they'll break from the heat.

Some commercial bakeries bake their bagels on **wooden boards** for the first 2 or 3 minutes, which gives them an overall even baking and nice crisp crust. These are lengths of 2-x-4's, available at any lumber yard, long enough to fit in your oven and hold 4 to 6 bagels. They may be covered on top with a length of burlap, stapled on, but that's not essential.

DIRECTIONS FOR MAKING BAGELS

The process is simple. Initially, the boiling procedure may seem strange, but once you've done it, you'll wonder why you hesitated. Just boil a pot of water as you would for spaghetti, and boil the shaped bagel for about 2 minutes, turning once. Your first few bagels may not come out round and smooth on top, but they'll taste good anyway. Be patient. The second batch will look better; by the third, you may think you're ready to go into business.

Briefly, these are the basic steps required to make bagels. We'll go into each in detail.

1. **Mix, knead and first rise:** Mix flour, water, salt, sugar (or malt or honey) and yeast, knead them and let the dough rise for about 1 hour. Mixing and kneading can be done in a bread machine, a food processor, a heavy duty mixer or by hand. This same procedure is used to prepare any yeast bread.
2. **Shape bagels:** Form the dough into the traditional bagel shape by rolling, poking a hole in a ball or using a bagel cutter.
3. **Second rise:** Allow a short rest and second rise period, about 20 minutes.
4. **Boil or "kettle":** Drop the bagels into boiling water for 1 to 3 minutes and drain. You can bake immediately, or refrigerate for 1 to 24 hours.

5. **Glaze and apply topping:** This step is not essential to the final product.
6. **Bake:** Bake in a preheated oven for 20 to 35 minutes.

STEP 1: MIX, KNEAD AND FIRST RISE

THE BREAD MACHINE

The bread machine yields excellent results every time when you use fresh ingredients and follow directions. Set the machine on "dough cycle," and let it produce a dough with the texture of velvet and the stiff consistency required.

When using a bread machine, add ingredients in the order recommended in your manufacturer's instructions. The recipes in this book have ingredients listed for machines that require adding liquids first and dry components last. Reverse the order for those that add dry ingredients first and wet ones last. Process on the "dough mode," or "program," or "mix bread cycle" or whatever it is termed by your machine's instructions. Allow dough to rise through the full first rise period after the kneading phase, between 35 minutes and 1 hour. On shorter cycles, and depending on weather and moisture of the ingredients, you may have to leave it in the machine for 10 or 15 minutes longer, or until the dough fills about 2/3 of the pan. Whole grain flours may require up to 1 to 2 hours for the first rise. Do not allow dough to bake in the machine.

Dry ingredients such as spices, cinnamon, nutmeg and finely chopped nuts are added with the flours at the beginning. Wet ingredients such as mashed bananas, applesauce, pumpkin, grated carrots and frozen berries are added with the liquids, but if you add more wet ingredients to the recipes in this book, their liquid content must replace an equal amount of liquid. Adding raisins and other dried fruits at the beginning is not recommended; most bread machines pulverize them so they're hardly visible in the finished bagel.

Check dough about 5 minutes after you have started the machine. The dough should form a nice round ball. If a ball doesn't form, and the mixture appears crumbly, add water, a tablespoon or less at a time, until the correct consistency is achieved. If dough looks too wet and formless, add flour, a tablespoon or less at a time, until dough forms a ball.

Add ingredients such as raisins, dates, chocolate chips and apple pieces about 5 to 8 minutes before the end of the kneading phase. Some machines beep to indicate the optimum time to add raisins or nuts. Check your manufacturer's instructions for the time required for each process in the dough cycle. If your machine does not provide this timed signal, determine the length of the kneading phase and set a timer for 5 minutes before the end; then open the machine and carefully add ingredients, being sure that they do not spill onto the heating elements. Ingredients can also be kneaded into the dough by hand after it is removed from the machine.

NOTE: When adding reconstituted dried foods to the dough in a bread machine (5 to 10 minutes before the end of the kneading phase), foods should be blotted very dry with a paper towel so that any retained liquid does not change the texture of the dough and inhibit it from rising properly.

A 60-minute rise period is ideal. It's OK to open the machine and quickly test the dough during the rise period. Gently push your finger into the dough, and if the dent remains, dough is ready. If the impression bounces back, let dough rise a few minutes longer and retest. Dough can become slack if it's allowed to rise too long. White flour rises highest. White flour combined with whole wheat, rye and oats will not rise as high. Generally, the darker the dough, the lower the rise and the longer it takes.

When ready, remove dough from the pan and proceed to *Step 2: Shape Bagels*, on page 20.

THE FOOD PROCESSOR

A food processor will knead dough ingredients very quickly and easily. It will reduce the process to a few minutes, even cutting down the time of a bread machine. Our testers found the results extremely reliable. One tester much preferred it to the bread machine because he was in charge all the way and never had a failure. By mixing and kneading in the food processor and allowing the dough to rise in the microwave, bagels can be ready for boiling in under a half hour. You can optionally use the microwave for the first rise for dough that has been mixed in the bread machine, by hand or with an electric mixer. Then work the flavoring ingredients into the dough after the first rise as you would for dough made in the bread machine. Either active dry yeast or fast-rising yeast can be used.

1. Warm ¼ of the liquid to 110°-115° in the microwave and add to yeast and sugar in a small cup. Mix gently and let it sit for 5 minutes. Prepare remaining liquid in a cup and make it very cool, right out of the refrigerator, or add an ice cube.

2. Put the metal cutting blade into the food processor bowl. Measure flour and salt and put them in the food processor bowl. Pulse two or three times, just enough to mix the flour and salt. Add any oil or butter and pulse until it disappears, two or three pulses.

    NOTE: Most food processors can mix 3¼ to 3½ cups flour. However, it's possible to mix a larger or double batch of dough. If the machine balks, it will stop automatically. Let it cool down and restart it. Or divide dough in half and continue processing each half separately. When mixed, knead the two batches together.

3. Pour yeast mixture into flour through the feeding tube and pulse for 5 or 10 seconds to combine. Add ice water or other cold liquid slowly through the feeding tube and pulse for another 5 or 10 seconds until dough forms a ball. Pulse a few more times to knead. When dough appears to come away from sides, it is ready.

4. Remove dough from the processor bowl and hand-knead to remove any gases. Let it rest for about 5 minutes. If it's not elastic enough, add a few more drops of water; if it's still sticky, add a sprinkle of flour until it is smooth, velvety and elastic. The first rise can be done in the microwave in about 15 minutes or in a bowl in a draft-free environment in about 1 hour. Microwave ovens vary in wattage, so the rise period and settings may vary. You may have to experiment.

    To use a microwave oven, after dough is kneaded, carefully remove it and the metal blade from the processor bowl. Form dough into a rectangle long enough to wrap once around the stem or center of the food processor bowl. Grease dough with oil or nonstick vegetable spray, but do not cover bowl. (Be sure the bowl has no metal parts.) Place the bowl in the microwave.

    Method 1: Microwave on LOW (30% power), or DEFROST (about 30%), for 1 minute. Let rest for 10 minutes. Repeat microwaving and resting 1 to 2 times, until dough has doubled in size. Test with your fingers until a dent remains. If the dent springs back and dough has not doubled, microwave once more for a few minutes until a dent does remain and dough appears doubled in size.

    Method 2: Or, place dough in the processor bowl as instructed. Position an 8-ounce microwave-safe cup filled with water in the back corner of the microwave. Cover the processor bowl lightly with a damp tea towel or plastic wrap and place it in the microwave on LOW (30% power) or DEFROST (about 30%) setting. Heat for 3 minutes, rest for 3 minutes, heat for 3 minutes and rest for 6 minutes, repeating the 3-minute heat and the 6-minute rest once or twice if necessary, until dough has doubled in bulk.

To allow dough to rise in a draft-free environment, place dough in a large bowl lightly oiled with vegetable oil. Turn dough so all surfaces are greased. Cover with plastic wrap sprayed with nonstick vegetable spray and let rise until doubled in bulk, about 1 to 2 hours.

Proceed to *Step 2: Shape Bagels*, on page 20.

THE HEAVY-DUTY MIXER WITH A DOUGH HOOK

A heavy-duty electric mixer with a dough hook will make short work of mixing small or large batches of dough quickly.

Combine the warm liquid (105° to 115°), syrup, honey or sugar, oil and yeast, and then add half the flour and all other dry ingredients. Add remaining flour until a ball forms.

The dough hook will do part or all of the kneading, which should take about 5 minutes. If dough begins to strain the machine, add more water so it becomes softer (check your manufacturer's directions; a heavy-duty mixer with a dough hook should have no problem kneading). When dough appears near desired consistency, remove it from the bowl and knead in extra dough until it forms a soft ball.

Follow the same first rise procedures as in the hand-mixing or food processor methods. If a fast-rising yeast is used, the first rise is not necessary.

Proceed to *Step 2: Shape Bagels*, on page 20.

BY HAND

Mix together warm water (110°-115°), yeast and 1 tsp. sugar and let stand for 5 minutes. In a large bowl, add remaining sugar, salt and 2 cups flour. Stir in yeast mixture. Add remaining flour, stirring to form dough.

Turn dough out onto a lightly floured board. Knead dough by hand, adding more flour as necessary, for 10 to 15 minutes until dough is smooth, satiny, stiff and elastic. Keep the board and your hands dusted with flour to prevent sticking.

Knead by pushing down on the dough with the palms of your hands, exerting pressure from your shoulders. Lift the dough from the top edge, turn it a quarter turn, fold it in half, press again, turn, fold, press and repeat the process until dough forms a cohesive ball. When dough is no longer sticky, stretch it to help develop elasticity. Knead a few more times. Drop it on your board, lift it, pick it up again and drop it again, continuing to stretch, drop and knead a few more times. If it becomes too stiff, add a few drops of water; if too sticky, add a little more flour. When optimally kneaded and shaped into a ball, dough will spring back when poked gently.

Place dough in a lightly greased bowl. Turn dough so all surfaces are greased. Cover with a sheet of plastic wrap sprayed with nonstick vegetable spray and let rise until doubled in bulk, about 1 hour. The test for proper rising, which about doubles the mass of dough in size, is to poke two fingers lightly and quickly about ½ inch into dough. If the dent stays, the dough is doubled.

Proceed to *Step 2: Shape Bagels*.

STEP 2: SHAPE BAGELS

Prepare baking sheets by lightly greasing them with nonstick vegetable spray, or with a little vegetable oil spread with your fingertips or waxed paper.

Reach into the bread machine pan and pull dough out (if it is slightly sticky, dip your fingers into flour first). Some machines punch dough down automatically at the end of the rise cycle, and just the act of removing the dough from the pan is usually adequate to remove gases, but you may need to punch dough down to remove any remaining air. Or, remove dough from bowl or food processor bowl and punch down.

Knead dough once or twice and let it rest for 5 minutes. If dough is still a little too wet and sticky, lightly flour the bread board or your hands and knead dough manually, until it has a smooth, elastic consistency. Bagel dough should be stiff but elastic; if it's too stiff, sprinkle a little water on it or moisten your hands and knead the moisture into dough. After you've made one or two batches of bagels, you'll get the feeling of the ideal consistency.

Roll and pull dough into a rectangle about 10 x 14 inches for a 1-pound recipe and 14 x 18 inches for a 1½-pound recipe, and let it rest for 5 minutes. Sprinkle with dried fruits, nuts, vegetables, seeds, spices, chocolate, or any combination of flavorings. Roll dough into a log and knead the ingredients into the dough for a minute or so.

The dough should weigh a little more than the size recipe you're using. Divide dough into pieces depending on the size bagel you want. A 1½-pound recipe yields 8 to 12 finished bagels, each weighing 2 to 3 ounces, measuring about 4 inches across. Use a food scale if you want consistency, or measure with a ruler. Cut smaller pieces for mini bagels. Knead in added ingredients well before shaping each bagel. You can also divide dough and add different ingredients to each part so you get a varied batch of bagels from one recipe.

Shape using any of the following methods:

- *the hole in the middle method*: Roll each piece of dough into a ball, poke a floured finger through the center to form the hole, and then shape top and smooth sides. Moisten your finger with water, if necessary to smooth. Pull gently to enlarge the hole. The resulting bagel is smooth and there is no joint.

  OR, press the round on your floured board. Using the index fingers of both hands, poke a hole and pull dough until the hole is large, and then round out the bagel and smooth the top and edges.

- *the hula hoop around the finger method*: Create a circle without a joint by flattening a ball of dough slightly into a round shape, folding the bottom edge under and smoothing it until it looks like a mushroom top. With a floured index finger, make a hole in the center of the circle from the bottom up. Twirl the circle around your index finger, or two fingers, like a hula hoop, to widen the hole. Pull out and shape the round.

- *the rope method*: Roll each piece of dough into a rope by rolling it on the bread board or between your hands. Wrap the rope around four fingers, overlap and join the ends, and turn the circle inside out. Until you get this hand movement down pat, you may have to moisten the ends to hold them together. Initially, the length may be lumpy and the joint will show. It takes practice.

  OR, roll dough into 30-inch lengths, cut each length into thirds (each 10 inches long) and join the ends. If you become proficient at this hand-made method, make 10-inch marks on the edge of your bread board so your bagels will be a consistent size.

- *bagel cutter method*: Roll dough out to a flat shape about ½-inch thick. Cut with a bagel cutter and smooth the tops over the sides so they're rounded, using a little water on your finger to smooth, if necessary. Knead scraps again, reroll and cut into as many more bagels as there is dough. If you don't have a bagel cutter, use a wide champagne glass to cut the outside. Cut the inside hole with the edge of a cordial glass or the small end of a measuring jigger. Any leftover dough can be rolled into two strips and made into a *Bagel Twist* (see page 52), sealing ends with a dab of water so they don't untwist while boiling and baking.

Place shaped bagels on the greased baking sheet for the second rise, spacing them at least an inch apart to allow for the second rise. Proceed to *Step 3: Second Rise*.

STEP 3: SECOND RISE

During the second rising of the dough, the bagels will puff up on the greased baking sheet. Cover them with a length of plastic wrap sprayed with nonstick cooking spray or with a very lightly dampened light cloth such as a tea towel. Place them in a draft-free location and let them rise at room temperature until puffy, about 20 minutes.

NOTE: Bagels can be refrigerated at this point, should you decide to boil and bake them later, or the next morning. Leave covered so they do not dry out. Remove from the refrigerator and allow to warm slightly while you boil water and preheat the oven.

The second rise can be speeded up by using the microwave. Fill a 2-cup microwave-proof measuring cup with water and bring water to a boil. Place in a corner of the microwave. Place the baking sheet of covered bagels in the microwave and close the door, but do not turn on the microwave! The bagels should rise in about 6 minutes. (It won't matter if the sheet is metal because you don't turn on the oven.)

Or, spray shaped dough tops with water. Place bagels on a microwave-safe surface and heat in the microwave on LOW or DEFROST setting for 3 minutes; rest for 3 minutes. Repeat heating and resting until bagels are puffy.

Proceed to *Step 4: Boil or "Kettle."*

STEP 4: BOIL OR "KETTLE"

Fill a 4- to 6-quart soup pot with water 3 to 4 inches deep. Water alone can be used, or add 2 tbs. malt syrup, honey or sugar.

Preheat the oven to 400°, so it's ready when you're through boiling the bagels.

Drop bagels one at a time into boiling water. Boil about 4 at a time or only so many that they float freely and do not crowd; they will expand further in the hot water. The bagel may sink to the bottom for a few seconds, and then float to the surface. Simmer for 30 seconds to 1 minute on each side, turning with a slotted spatula. Remove and place on a lightly greased rack or a lightly floured tea towel for a few minutes to drain.

HINT: Put the top side of the bagel down into water first, and then turn over. When you remove them, the bagels will be top side up and slide off your spatula for draining and adding toppings.

When cool enough to handle, proceed to *Step 5: Glaze and Apply Topping*, or if you omit this step, proceed to *Step 6: Bake*.

STEP 5, OPTIONAL: GLAZE AND APPLY TOPPING

GLAZES

Brush tops with glaze either before placing them in the oven or about 5 minutes into the baking and again about 5 minutes before end of baking. I've tried all the glazes listed below on the same bagels in one batch, using white flour bagels and whole grain flour bagels. Despite claims in some cookbooks that different glazes yield different shades and crustiness, I found no appreciable difference in either color or texture of the crusts when applied to bagels. You may have a different result.

Water glaze: A spray or brushing with room-temperature tap water will yield a subtle glaze similar to using the steam baking method, page 30. Try brushing some bagels at the beginning of the baking, some 5 minutes after and some near the end, and compare the differences.

Nonstick vegetable spray glaze: An easy, quick, effective, low-calorie glaze is a spray of nonstick vegetable spray. It goes on more evenly than using a brush, yet yields an even glaze. Spray before placing in oven, and again about 5 minutes before baking time is completed.

Vegetable oil glaze: Use a pastry brush to coat bagels lightly.

Melted butter or margarine glaze: This glaze produces the same effect as vegetable oil. Watch the bagels carefully so they don't burn.

Egg glaze #1: Mix together 1 egg white, 1 egg yolk or 1 whole egg with 1 to 2 tbs. water, milk or cream.

Egg glaze #2: Lightly beat 1 egg white. You can brush it on the bagels either before they are put in the oven or 5 minutes after the baking has begun, and again 5 minutes before the baking is finished.

Cornstarch glaze: Dissolve 2 tbs. cornstarch in 1/4 cup cold water. Bring 1 cup water to a boil and whisk the dissolved solution into the boiling water until it thickens. This cornstarch mixture can be kept in the refrigerator for several days. Brush it on the bagel tops at the beginning of the baking and again as you remove the bagels from the oven, for a very high shine.

TOPPINGS

A variety of toppings can be added to the bagel before baking, either directly to the dough after kettling, or after the bagel is glazed. Poppy seeds, sesame seeds, caraway seeds and coarse salt are easiest to use because they can be placed in a dish directly from the jar, and the bagel can be dipped into the dish; the seeds adhere to the moist dough. Or they can be sprinkled on top of the bagels just before baking, and pressed down lightly to adhere. I've seen bagels with sparse toppings and those that are covered from top and bottom. There's no right or wrong way.

- Add ½ cup finely chopped, lightly sautéed onions to the top of the bagels.
- Add ½ cup finely chopped raw onions to the top of the bagels; they will cook along with the bagels.
- Use dehydrated onion flakes or packaged onion soup that you have reconstituted with water, olive oil or vegetable oil. Use 1 tbs. dry product to ½ tbs. water or oil, and soak for 2 to 3 minutes.
- Mix together: ½ cup chopped yellow onions, 1 green onion (white part only), 2 tsp. olive oil, 2 tsp. poppy seeds.
- Sprinkle with garlic salt, finely chopped fresh garlic or garlic flakes.
- For the *Everything Bagel* (see page 85), combine ½ cup finely chopped

onions, 1 clove garlic, finely chopped, and ¼ cup sesame seeds. Sprinkle mixture on bagel tops before baking.

- Use ground caraway or whole caraway seeds. These are particularly good on rye bagels. They can be combined with the topping for the *Everything Bagel*.
- Sprinkle with red pepper flakes, adjusting the "heat" to your liking.
- Top with mixed fresh herbs, including parsley, chives and dill.
- Dip into or distribute about ¼ cup coarse salt or kosher salt on top of 1 batch of bagels just before baking.
- Poppy, caraway, sesame and celery seeds can be used directly from the jar. Just dip the bagels into a dish of seeds or sprinkle seeds on top.
- Toasting nuts before using them on (and in) bagels enhances their flavor. Walnuts, almonds, pecans or hazelnuts can be used on bagels as toppings and also added to the dough at the beginning or before they are shaped and rise the second time. To toast a small amount of nuts, spread them in a heavy sauté pan and shake or gently stir them over medium heat until lightly browned (6 to 10 minutes). Larger amounts can be spread on a baking sheet and baked for about 10 minutes in a 350° oven. Shake or stir them once or twice during baking.

- Sprinkle with rolled oats or multigrain cereal, which will brown while baking. Proceed to *Step 6: Bake*.

STEP 6: BAKE

Place bagels on a shelf just below the middle in a preheated 400° oven and bake for 20 to 25 minutes or until tops are a nice golden brown.

BAKING SURFACES

- *Bake the bagels on a baking sheet*. The easiest surface available to most home cooks is an aluminum cookie sheet or a flat Teflon-coated sheet pan. Coat with a little oil and sprinkle very lightly with yellow cornmeal to prevent bagels from sticking. Or line the pan with parchment paper; it eliminates the use of oil and cornmeal, and cleaning pans.

- *Bake the bagels on wooden boards* (see description on page 11). Place bagels on the boards bottom side up to yield a crusty bottom, and flip them off the board after 2 or 3 minutes onto a stone or sheet to continue baking.

- *Bake the bagels directly on a baking stone or tiles*. Place the stone or tiles on the lowest rack. Or line a baking sheet with the tiles and place that on the lowest rack. Preheat the oven, with stone or tiles inside, to 400° for 1 hour before baking. Sprinkle cornmeal on the stone or tiles. Transfer unbaked bagels to the hot surface with a wooden peel (a long-handled wooden paddle used in baking), or any flat instrument with a long handle so you don't burn yourself; wear heavy padded gloves.

Do not wash or immerse stone or tiles in cold water while they are hot; they may crack. Soak the cooled stone or tiles in cold water and scrape with a spatula. Do not use soap, as the surfaces tend to absorb soap, which will be imparted to the bagels. Stones and tiles will discolor, but that won't affect their baking ability. Don't place a hot stone directly on your kitchen counter; depending on the material, the heat could leave a mark.

Steam baking gives bagel tops a crisp crust and extra shine. Create steam during the first few seconds of the baking by spraying the sides of the preheated oven with water from a spray bottle when you place the bagels inside. Place a heavy pan in the lower part of the oven bottom while it is heating. Place the bagels in the oven and then pour cold water or a half dozen ice cubes into the pan.

STORING AND USING BAGELS

Bagels are best when they're eaten fresh from the oven while still warm. Because they usually don't contain egg or milk, they tend to dry out faster than breads that contain these ingredients. If you can't consume all the bagels in a reasonably short time, freezing them is recommended. It's smart to slice them horizontally before freezing so you can toast only half at a time, if you wish.

Thaw bagels on the kitchen counter in a plastic bag for about 15 minutes or toast frozen bagel halves directly from the freezer. Or zap them in the microwave for about 1 minute on DEFROST and then toast them until lightly browned on top. Microwaving too long will make them tough.

What if a few bagels get stale? Put them in your blender or food processor and grind them into breadcrumbs. None of the tasty bread need ever go to waste!

HANDY TABLE OF EQUIVALENTS

Yeast measurements

1 package + 1/4 tsp. dry yeast	=	1/4 oz.
2 1/2 tsp.	=	1 package + 1/4 tsp. active dry yeast
1 package dry yeast	=	1 cake* (0.6 oz.) fresh yeast

Cake yeast is not recommended for bread machines.

Basic measurements

1 1/2 tsp.	=	1/2 tbs.
3 tsp.	=	1 tbs.
4 tbs.	=	1/4 cup
5 1/3 tbs.	=	1/3 cup
16 tbs.	=	1 cup

Eighth measures are often used for measuring liquids

1/8 cup	=	2 tbs.
3/8 cup	=	1/4 cup + 2 tbs.
5/8 cup	=	1/2 cup + 2 tbs.
7/8 cup	=	3/4 cup + 2 tbs.
1 1/8 cups	=	1 cup + 2 tbs.

1/3 cup measures are often used for measuring flours and other grains

1/3 cup	=	5 1/3 tbs.
2/3 cup	=	1/2 cup + 2 2/3 tbs.

INGREDIENTS

The home baker probably has most bagel ingredients in the pantry already. Most are available in supermarkets, health food stores, or from *Bagel Supply Sources*, page 164. Missing something? Most likely there are easy substitutes.

Bread flour: This flour is recommended for bagels because it has sufficient gluten to give a bagel its chewy crust. Bread flour absorbs a bit more liquid than all-purpose or unbleached flour and yields a more "elastic" feeling when kneaded. Bread flour, sometimes labeled "high-protein flour," may require more kneading than all-purpose flour. Unbleached flour can be substituted for bread flour.

Whole wheat flour: Whole wheat flour is light brown in color and contains all natural nutrients. It's the most popular addition to white flour. Whole wheat flour should not exceed 50% of the total flour content. Whole wheat, and other whole grain flours, do not have as much gluten and will not rise as high as white flours. One cup whole wheat flour is equal to 7/8 cup white flour. If you're replacing 1/2 cup white flour, use 1/2 cup plus 1 tbs. whole wheat flour. Whole wheat flour may also be sold as graham flour in health food stores. A good substitute for whole wheat flour is spelt flour, a grain that is easier to digest than wheats and often used by people with gluten intolerance.

Rye flour: Rye flour can yield a variety of flavors and textures. Types include dark rye, light rye and coarse rye. The amount of rye flour also controls the taste. Stone-ground rye, sometimes available in health food stores, has the best flavor. Pumpernickel flour is medium-ground rye flour, and it is labeled medium rye on commercial packages.

Oats: Use rolled oats, not instant. This is the same product sold for oatmeal cereal with its flaky consistency. Oat bran and oat flour can be substituted for rolled oats in smaller quantities (1 cup oats equals about 2/3 cup oat bran or oat flour). Oat flour can be purchased in health food stores or by mail order. Rolled oats can be ground into oat flour in a blender or food processor.

Bran: Unprocessed Miller's bran is a natural grain product high in dietary fiber. It can be used interchangeably with processed bran flakes. Both can be found with breakfast cereals in supermarkets. You need 1 cup bran flakes to yield about 2/3 cup bran.

Cornmeal: Cornmeal is ground from corn kernels; the most common cornmeal is yellow, but there are also white and blue cornmeals. It is used in many recipes along with other flours. A thin sprinkling of cornmeal is used on the baking sheet or baking stone to provide a nonstick baking surface for the bagels.

Vital wheat gluten: This is the natural protein derived from wheat. Adding it to rye, whole wheat and other whole grains increases the protein value of bread and provides the elasticity in the dough to allow the yeast to develop gases, at the same time holding them in to yield a less dense, lighter dough with greater volume. The fine, powdery product can be purchased in health food stores. Recommended additions are 1½ tsp. per 1 cup flour for whole grain breads and 1 tsp. per 1 cup flour for white breads. Use a little more gluten when raisins, nuts, seeds and brans are used. Gluten should be well mixed in with flour. I have suggested that vital gluten is optional, but once you begin using it, it may become essential: testing showed that breads and bagels with vital gluten added were lighter and tastier than those made without it.

Yeast: Yeast is responsible for the density of a bagel, and often the difference in regional recipes. For all recipes, active dry yeast is assumed and amounts given are for a moderately dense bagel as close as possible to the accepted standard of a New York-style bagel. Yeast is composed of thousands of tiny living plants which, when given moisture, warmth and "food," will grow and give off a gas (carbon dioxide); it is that gas that makes dough rise.

Yeast is available in active dry and in compressed fresh forms. One package or 1 scant tablespoon of active dry yeast is equivalent to 1 cake (¾ ounces) of compressed yeast. Cake yeast is not recommended for bread machines, but could be used to make bagels with other methods. There is also fast-rising yeast sold under different product names such Rapid Rise, Instant, 50% faster, Quick Rise, or SAF-Instant, which can be converted to work as active dry yeast. Reduce the amount of fast-rising yeast by 25% when substituting it for active dry yeast and reduce the first rising time. To convert fast-rising yeast to active dry yeast, add 1 teaspoon of sugar to ½ cup water per 1 packet of yeast.

Buy and use yeast before its life potency date expires; all bottles and packages of yeast are dated. For denser bagels, reduce the yeast called for in the recipe by ½ teaspoon. For spongier, less dense bagels, increase yeast by ¼ to ½ teaspoon.

Malt syrup: Malt syrup, made from barley, helps give bagels their unique appeal. Malt assists with browning, and feeds the yeast. It's available in jars where health food supplies are sold (used as a sweetener) or from stores that sell beer brewing supplies. Malt powder can be substituted in amounts comparable to liquid malt. Honey, molasses, or brown or white sugar can be substituted for malt syrup.

Darkening agents: Baker's caramel, also called blackjack, is a natural coloring agent that bakers use to give dark breads, such as pumpernickels and ryes, their hearty hues. Essentially, it is burnt or caramelized sugar, and it resembles dark-brewed coffee in appearance. Substitutes are unsweetened cocoa and instant coffee crystals. Another substitute is Kitchen Bouquet, a gravy-coloring agent, available in the grocery soup or flavorings section. It does contain extra salt, so it may slightly alter the bagel's flavor.

Water: Many bread recipes call for tap water, which is more to indicate water temperature than quality. Water temperature should be about 105° to 115°F — the temperature range needed to activate yeast. In cold weather, tap water may be too cold. A thermometer will help determine water temperature. If necessary, warm the water slightly in a microwave or in a pot for a few seconds to bring it to the proper temperature. I like to use bottled water because water where I live tastes so bad I won't drink it straight or use it for coffee. So why put it in bread? It also provides a constant for testing and comparing bagels in different cities.

Tap water can be used for boiling the bagels. Someone told me that soft water yields soft bagels and hard water yields hard bagels, but that's not so. There's also a rumor that New York bagels are different and better than all others because of the Hudson River water. This has been debunked by every bagel baker with whom I spoke (except those in New York). Besides, New York bagels differ from each other by bakeries.

Eggs: Traditional water bagels do not call for eggs, but many recipes can benefit from the addition of eggs and, of course, they're used in egg bagels. Egg bagels generally are softer than water bagels and the dough tends to rise more. Use fresh whole eggs or substitute 2 egg whites for 1 egg, or ¼ cup egg substitute for 1 egg.

Salt: Any commercial table salt can be used. Kosher salt and coarse salt are used as a topping.

Shortenings and oils: Vegetable oils used in bagel recipes, such as canola oil, peanut oil, corn oil and similar natural oils, tenderize the bread, give it flavor, improve the texture and add preserving qualities. The traditional Jewish bagel does not have oil, but many people like the flavor and softer texture that results when oil has been used. It's strictly optional. Nonstick vegetable sprays can be used for greasing the pan as well as for adding a glaze to the bagel top.

ADDING INGREDIENTS FOR FLAVOR AND TEXTURE

The bagel flavor depends largely on the freshness, quality and amount of added ingredients. Be generous with dried fruits, especially those that you work in before shaping. Use them in raisin-sized chunks rather than finely chopping them, so you get a substantial taste when you bite into the bagel. Almost every kind of fruit is now available dried from specialty food shops, or by mail.

Be creative. Combine ingredients to create your individualized bagel flavor combinations. Use dried fruits for most additions and experiment with fresh fruits. Canned and frozen fruits do not work well; they add too much liquid and often discolor the dough. Canned olives and chilies such as jalapeños are fine if they are well drained and blotted almost dry on paper towels before adding.

PROBLEM-SOLVING

I have to stop in the middle of making bagels. What should I do?

Dough can be refrigerated at any time after the first rise, and removed from the refrigerator to continue the process. Dough can be frozen at any stage after the first rise, and then thawed and the process resumed. When storing dough in the freezer or refrigerator, shape it into a flat disk, seal it in a locking plastic freezer bag or wrap it in airtight heavy-duty aluminum foil, to keep it from drying out. Label and date the package. It can remain for about 1 week in the refrigerator, and for several weeks in the freezer.

The flour sometimes attracts pests.

Place a couple of bay leaves in flour containers or bags to ward off any bugs. Small bags can be placed in the freezer overnight, or longer, to kill any lurking larvae. Freezing or refrigerating flour will keep it fresh longer; allow it to warm to room temperature before using.

I can hear the bread machine working, but nothing is moving.

If nothing is happening, you probably forgot to insert the dough mixing blade into the pan. Always replace it correctly in the pan as soon as you've washed the pan.

Dough is wet and sticky, and fails to form a ball in the machine.

There is probably too much liquid. Add flour a tablespoon or less at a time until a ball forms.

The dough in the machine looks dry, and is in small clumps.

There is not enough liquid. Add liquid a tablespoon or less at a time until a ball forms.

The bagels taste strange.

Forget to add one or more ingredients? Or did you add the wrong ones? Organize your baking shelf so ingredients are in the order required by the machine manufacturer. Take them all out when you begin, and put each one back as soon as you've used it.

Bagel bottoms are burned.

Using a thin aluminum cookie sheet or aluminum foil? Bagels tend to bake hotter and faster than on Teflon-coated baking sheets. Try a lower temperature, a longer baking time and a darker baking surface than shiny aluminum. Place the pan just below the middle of the oven, not at the bottom rack position. Also, check your oven's temperature with an oven thermometer. Or adjust the baking time and temperature.

The bagels seem too dense, and tough.

Boil the bagels too long? Boiling too long can make the dough dense and tough. There may also be mixing problems: too much flour or too much whole grain flour will make the dough heavy and dense. Measure carefully. Add gluten to dough and extra liquid to dough. Weather can be a factor, too.

Dough was improperly kneaded.

This is more likely to happen when kneading by hand or with a food processor or heavy-duty mixer. Dough must be worked long enough to activate the gluten and make the dough elastic. Stretching dough while kneading is necessary for activating gluten.

Dough doesn't rise.

Is the yeast old or was it improperly stored? Yeast should be used before the expiration date on the package and, once opened, it should be refrigerated.

How do you store bagels properly?

Bagels stale rapidly. They should either be eaten while they're fresh or stored in the freezer. Defrost them quickly (under a minute) on LOW in a microwave, or at room temperature, and then toast. Or cut in half before freezing, and toast the halves directly from the freezer.

Honey and molasses are hard to measure, because they stick to the spoon.

When recipes call for both oil and sticky sweeteners, such as malt syrup, honey or molasses, measure the oil first and use the same spoon for the sweetener; it will slide off the oiled spoon easily.

I live in a high altitude.

All bread books caution that in areas that are 3,000 feet or more above sea level, high altitude adjustments may be required. There are no exact rules and some experimentation should be expected. I tested six basic recipes at 5,000 feet (Albuquerque, New Mexico, in winter) and found no consistent difference in the amounts of ingredients needed. Some recipes required a little extra water, but that may have been for a variety of reasons. Even the boiling time remained consistent, although some people who live at high altitudes reported that they boiled the bagels for up to 6 minutes. Longer than that made them as hard as rocks.

BASIC BAGEL RECIPES

BASIC NEW YORK WATER BAGELS

This is the bagel that launched millions of clones and has become the standard by which other bagels are compared. In reality, all bagels boiled in water are "water bagels."

	1 pound	1½ pound
water	¾ cup	1⅛ cups
vegetable oil	1 tbs.	1 tbs.
malt syrup, molasses or white sugar	1 tbs.	2 tbs.
salt	¾ tsp.	1 tsp.
bread flour	2¾ cups	3⅓ cups
active dry yeast	1½ tsp.	2 tsp.

Glaze, optional: nonstick vegetable spray, Mazola oil, or egg yolk beaten with 1 tbs. water

Suggested toppings: poppy seeds, sesame seeds, onions, garlic salt or kosher salt

BASIC WHOLE WHEAT BAGELS

Whole wheat added to white flour changes everything: the color becomes slightly tan, the texture is coarser and the flavor has a slightly nutty quality.

	1 pound	1½ pound
water	¾ cup	1⅛ cups
vegetable oil	1 tbs.	1 tbs.
malt syrup or brown sugar	1 tbs.	2 tbs.
salt	¾ tsp.	1¼ tsp.
whole wheat flour	¾ cup	1 cup
bread flour	2 cups	2⅓ cups
vital gluten, optional	2 tsp.	1 tbs.
active dry yeast	1½ tsp.	2½ tsp.

Glaze, optional: 1 egg white beaten with 1 tbs. water
Suggested toppings: poppy seeds, sesame seeds or celery seeds

BASIC JEWISH RYE BAGELS

Rye bagels have that wonderful old-world aroma, and when they're fresh from the oven, their taste is tantalizing. Use caraway seeds in the flour mixture and for the topping. Allow extra rising time.

	1 pound	**1½ pound**
water	⅞ cup	1⅓ cups
vegetable oil	1 tbs.	2 tbs.
malt syrup, molasses or honey	2 tbs.	3 tbs.
salt	¾ tsp.	1 tsp.
unsweetened cocoa powder	¾ tbs.	1 tbs.
caraway seeds	¼ cup	⅔ cup
cornmeal	¼ cup	⅓ cup
light rye flour	½ cup	¾ cup
bread flour	1¾ cups	2¼ cups
vital gluten, optional	2 tsp.	4 tsp.
active dry yeast	1½ tsp.	2½ tsp.

Suggested topping: caraway seeds

BASIC PUMPERNICKEL BAGELS

Pumpernickel is a coarse, dark bread made with white flour, a high proportion of dark or light rye flour and a small amount of wheat flour. Cocoa or coffee is added as a coloring agent. Allow 45 minutes to 1 hour extra for the first rise because the whole grain flours lack the gluten of white flours. Vital gluten will make the bread less dense.

	1 pound	**1½ pound**
water	⅞ cup	1⅓ cups
vegetable oil	1 tbs.	1 tbs.
malt syrup, molasses or brown sugar	1 tbs.	2 tbs.
unsweetened cocoa powder or instant coffee crystals	1 tbs.	1½ tbs.
salt	¾ tsp.	1¼ tsp.
dark rye flour	½ cup	½ cup
whole wheat flour	¼ cup	1 cup
bread flour	1½ cups	2 cups
vital gluten	1 tbs.	4½ tsp.
active dry yeast	1½ tsp.	2½ tsp.

Suggested toppings: **celery seeds, dried onion flakes or rolled oats**

BASIC OAT BAGELS

Oat flour is available in grocery and health food stores. If not available, make oat flour in your food processor, or substitute uncooked oats (not instant) in the amounts given. Allow extra time for the first rise.

	1 pound	**1½ pound**
water	¾ cup	1¼ cups
vegetable oil	1 tbs.	2 tbs.
malt syrup, molasses or		
brown sugar	1 tbs.	2 tbs.
salt	¾ tsp.	1 tsp.
oat flour	½ cup	1 cup
or rolled oats	⅔ cup	1⅓ cups
whole wheat flour	¼ cup	½ cup
bread flour	2 cups	2 cups
vital gluten, optional	2 tsp.	1 tbs.
active dry yeast	1½ tsp.	2½ tsp.

Suggested toppings: **finely chopped almonds, pecans or walnuts; whole raw pine nuts, sunflower seeds or rolled oats**

BASIC EGG BAGELS

*The usual bagel texture and glossy crust are achieved by boiling the egg bagel. However, some people prefer a soft dough bagel that tastes more like regular white bread. For a soft bagel, use the same recipe, but do not boil the bagels in water. Instead, after they have completed the second rise, add an egg glaze and bake them in a 350° oven for 20 minutes or until they are a nice golden brown. (Also see **Easter Egg Bagels With Candy Sprinkles**, page 93.)*

	1 pound	**1½ pound**
water	¾ cup	1 cup
egg (or 2 egg whites)	1	1
vegetable oil	1½ tbs.	2 tbs.
sugar	1 tbs.	2 tbs.
salt	¾ tsp.	1 tsp.
bread flour	2½ cups	3⅓ cups
active dry yeast	1½ tsp.	2 tsp.

Glaze, optional: **spray with water**
Suggested toppings: **sesame seeds, poppy seeds or sunflower seeds**

THE MINI BAGEL

Use any bagel recipe for mini bagels, which measure about 2 inches in diameter. Divide 1-pound recipes into 10 to 12 pieces. Divide 1½-pound recipes into 12 to 15 pieces. Shape, leaving a large center hole, as the holes tend to close up as the bagels rise and bake. Bake for 15 to 20 minutes at 400°. Watch them carefully while baking so they don't become too brown.

THE BAGEL STICK

The bagel stick is shaped like a short, fat breadstick instead of the usual bagel shape. It can be served plain or covered with seeds. It's similar to the garlic or salt breadstick, only chewier like a bagel, rather than crisp like a breadstick. Use the *Basic New York Water Bagels* recipe on page 45. After rising, roll the dough into a flat rectangle, spread with toppings, cut into strips and shape into rounded lengths with smooth ends; 6 inches is a good length. Then proceed with the second rise, kettling and baking. Bagel sticks can be coated with seeds such as poppy, sesame, celery or caraway before they are baked. Minced onions and kosher salt are favorites, too.

If you like a softer dough, make the sticks with the egg recipe, and dip them into finely chopped walnuts, almonds, pecans, pine nuts or mixed nuts.

THE CHURRO STICK

The churro stick is a variation of both the breadstick and the dessert-like Mexican churro. The churro is a long roll of soft pastry dough, fried and dipped in sugar. Instead, make the bagel stick as directed on page 51, and roll it in a mixture of sugar and cinnamon. It's not greasy and it is much lower in calories than the churro.

THE BAGEL TWIST

The bagel twist, made with water bagel dough or egg dough, looks like a miniature challah, except that only 2 lengths of dough are twisted together (challahs use 3 strands for braiding.) Roll out 10-inch lengths of dough about the thickness of a pen. Seal one end of each together with a dab of water if necessary. Then twist the lengths and pinch and seal at the other end. Let them rise the second time; then boil and sprinkle tops with poppy or sesame seeds before baking.

THE TWIST WITH A TWIST

For a variation on the bagel twist, use two types of dough, a dark pumpernickel and a white dough, for an interesting "color twist."

THE MARBLED BAGEL

Use the two-color dough concept, as in *The Twist With a Twist*, page 52, and form them together carefully to make single bagels. The marbled bagel is a delicious and attractive addition to a platter filled with single-color bagels. Adding a glaze makes this gourmet bagel as pretty as a picture and delicious, as well.

THE PARTY BAGEL

Another popular bagel variation is an oversized party bagel, which can measure as large as the pot you have in which to boil it. Some bagel bakeries make them from 3 to 6½ pounds. For a bagel larger than the 1-pound, 1½-pound or 2-pound capacity of a bread machine, combine two or more recipes. Refrigerate one while the other is rising. Or prepare with an electric mixer or by hand. The large party bagel will need to be boiled for about 3 to 5 minutes on each side and baked until nicely browned. Poppy seed topping adds to its attractive appearance.

When baked, cut it horizontally through the center and stuff it with a selection of deli meats, cheeses, or lox and cream cheese, and garnish the top with tomatoes, onion rings and olives. Cut into pie-shaped wedges for serving.

BIALYS

While a bialy is not a bagel, it is so closely related, and so much a part of the Jewish bread culture, that omitting it from a book on bagels would be a major gaffe. What is a bialy? It's a circle of soft dough with a center indentation containing a filling. The traditional filling is a mixture of mixed onions, poppy seeds and vegetable oil. Today, bialys can be purchased with different fillings.

Their origin is attributed to a Jewish baker from the Polish town of Bialystock, who served in the army in central Asia. He tasted one of their pastries, improvised and brought the recipe to America when he immigrated. Bialys are made with bagel dough, but they are not boiled. A softer version can be made with all-purpose flour. Try the recipe both ways and decide for yourself.

	1 pound	**1½ pound**
water	¾ cup	1⅛ cups
sugar	2 tsp.	1 tbs.
salt	⅔ tsp.	¾ tsp.
bread flour or all-purpose flour	3 cups	3½ cups
yeast	1½ tsp.	2 tsp.

Upon completion of the dough cycle, remove dough and punch down. Rest the dough for 10 minutes, and then form it into 8 to 10 equal balls. Flatten each ball with a rolling pin to a 4-inch-diameter circle about ⅛-inch thick and place on a greased baking sheet lightly sprinkled with cornmeal. Cover with plastic wrap sprayed with nonstick food spray and allow to rise until puffy. Mix filling ingredients together. Make an indentation in the center of each ball with your thumbs or the bottom of a small shot glass. Dribble a tablespoon of filling into the hole. Bake in a preheated 400° oven for 20 to 25 minutes or until lightly browned. Glaze before baking (see pages 25-26 for suggested glazes).

ONION-POPPY SEED FILLING

3 tbs. minced onion or reconstituted onion flakes
1 tbs. poppy seeds

1 tsp. vegetable oil
¼ tsp. garlic salt
¼ tsp. kosher or coarse salt

SWEET CENTER FILLING

½ cup chopped dried fruit: apricots, raisins, prunes or dates
¼ cup chopped pecans or walnuts

½ tsp. cinnamon
¼ cup melted butter or margarine, or vegetable oil

BIALY PIZZA

Some traditionalist is sure to be offended by this title and ethnic combination, but it's delicious.

Double or triple the size of the *Bialy* circle, page 54, and roll out to a 5-, 6- or 8-inch diameter, depending on the size you want. Allow to rise the second time on a greased baking pan. Flatten, pressing down the center and leaving a 1-inch rim. Fill with onion or poppy seeds, or pizza sauce and veggies. Some bakers embellish the centers with anything that appeals to their customers, including pizza sauce with onions and green peppers.

Bake on a baking stone or on a cookie sheet at 400°, but allow extra baking time for the larger round than you would for the smaller bialy. Cut into wedges and serve as you would a pizza.

FRUIT, NUT AND SPICE-FLAVORED BAGELS

APPLE PECAN BAGELS

These are easy to make and very tasty. The applesauce and apple provide the liquid.

	1 pound	**1½ pound**
applesauce	¾ cup	⅝ cup
medium apple, cut into small pieces	1	1
vegetable oil	1 tbs.	1 tbs.
honey, malt syrup or brown sugar	1 tbs.	2 tbs.
salt	¾ tsp.	1 tsp.
cornmeal	⅛ cup	⅛ cup
whole wheat flour	½ cup	⅝ cup
bread flour	2 cups	2¾ cups
active dry yeast	1½ tsp.	2½ tsp.

Add at raisin/nut beep, 5 minutes before end of kneading phase, or work into dough:

pecans, coarsely chopped	½ cup	⅝ cup

APPLE, BRAN AND WALNUT BAGELS

Be creative with other nuts and dried fruits to vary this hearty bagel.

	1 pound	1½ pound
water	½ cup	1¼ cups
applesauce	¾ cup	1 cup
malt syrup or molasses	1 tbs.	2 tbs.
brown sugar	½ tsp.	¾ tsp.
medium apple, cut into small pieces	1	1
salt	¾ tsp.	1 tsp.
cornmeal	⅛ cup	⅛ cup
Miller's bran	½ cup	⅝ cup
bread flour	2 cups	2¾ cups
vital gluten, optional	2 tsp.	1 tbs.
active dry yeast	1½ tsp.	2½ tsp.

Add at raisin/nut beep, 5 minutes before end of kneading phase, or work into dough:

walnuts, coarsely chopped	½ cup	⅝ cup
raisins or dried currants, optional	¼ cup	¼ cup

BANANA, APPLE AND RAISIN BAGELS

With a blender, puree 3 red Delicious apples, cored and diced with the skin on, 2 sliced bananas, and ½ cup of any fruit juice or yogurt. Apple skins will leave a red fleck in the bagels.

	1 pound	1½ pound
water	¼ cup	¼ cup
banana-apple puree	½ cup	⅞ cup
vegetable oil	1 tbs.	1 tbs.
malt syrup or honey	1 tbs.	2 tbs.
salt	¾ tsp.	1 tsp.
cinnamon	1½ tsp.	2 tsp.
whole wheat flour	¾ cup	⅝ cup
bread flour	2 cups	2¾ cups
vital gluten, optional	2 tsp.	1 tbs.
active dry yeast	1½ tsp.	2½ tsp.

Add at raisin/nut beep, 5 minutes before end of kneading phase, or work into dough:
dark or golden raisins, or		
combination	½ cup	¾ cup

OLD-FASHIONED RAISIN CINNAMON BAGELS

The familiar, or old-fashioned, raisin cinnamon white bagel is a "can't miss" appetite-pleaser. Knead in another tablespoon or so of cinnamon before shaping the bagel for a marbleized look.

	1 pound	**1½ pound**
water	¾ cup	1¼ cups
vegetable oil	1 tbs.	2 tbs.
malt syrup, molasses or white sugar	1 tbs.	2 tbs.
salt	¾ tsp.	1 tsp.
cinnamon	1½ tsp.	2 tsp.
bread flour	2¾ cups	3⅓ cups
active dry yeast	1½ tsp.	2 tsp.

Add at raisin/nut beep, 5 minutes before end of kneading phase, or work into dough:

dark or golden raisins	½ cup	¾ cup

BANANA, PEANUT BUTTER AND RAISIN BAGELS

Check about 5 minutes after the machine has started, and if the dough appears too moist, add flour a tablespoon or less at a time until dough is the right consistency. Use well-ripened bananas when bananas are called for.

	1 pound	1½ pound
water	¼ cup	¼ cup
banana, mashed	¼ cup	⅝ cup
peanut butter, smooth or crunchy	½ cup	½ cup
malt syrup or honey	1 tbs.	2 tbs.
salt	¾ tsp.	1 tsp.
bread flour	2¾ cups	3⅓ cups
active dry yeast	1½ tsp.	2 tsp.

Add at raisin/nut beep, 5 minutes before end of kneading phase, or work into dough:

dark or golden raisins, or combination	½ cup	¾ cup

BANANA WHOLE WHEAT BAGELS

This healthy, delicious combination is a big hit. Add nuts for a variation.

	1 pound	**1½ pound**
water	½ cup	¾ cup
banana, sliced	½ cup	¾ cup
vegetable oil	1 tbs.	1 tbs.
malt syrup or brown sugar	1 tbs.	2 tbs.
salt	¾ tsp.	1¼ tsp.
cornmeal	¼ cup	¼ cup
whole wheat flour	¾ cup	1 cup
bread flour	1¾ cups	2⅓ cups
vital gluten, optional	2 tsp.	1 tbs.
active dry yeast	1½ tsp.	2½ tsp.

VARIATION: BANANA NUT WHOLE WHEAT BAGELS

Add at raisin/nut beep, 5 minutes before end of kneading phase, or work into dough:

whole raw pine nuts or walnuts, chopped	½ cup	¾ cup

MIXED DRIED FRUIT BAGELS

Adding a mixture of dried fruit to a whole wheat bagel results in a colorful, delicious medley of flavors. Cut fruits into small pieces (or buy them precut) and work them into dough as you shape it.

	1 pound	**1½ pound**
water	¾ cup	1⅛ cups
malt syrup or brown sugar	1 tbs.	2 tbs.
vegetable oil	1 tbs.	1 tbs.
salt	¾ tsp.	1¼ tsp.
cinnamon	1½ tsp.	1¾ tsp.
nutmeg	1½ tsp.	1¾ tsp.
whole wheat flour	¾ cup	1 cup
bread flour	2 cups	2⅓ cups
vital gluten, optional	2 tsp.	1 tbs.
active dry yeast	1½ tsp.	2½ tsp.

Add at raisin/nut beep, 5 minutes before end of kneading phase, or work into dough:

mixed dried fruits, cut into pea-sized pieces	⅜ cup	⅝ cup

BLUEBERRY BRAN BAGELS

Blueberry bagels are one of the most popular favors sold by bagel shops. Their flavor is wonderful, and the added blue color is appetizing.

	1 pound	**1½ pound**
water	1 cup	1⅛ cups
vegetable oil	1 tbs.	1 tbs.
malt syrup or brown sugar	1 tbs.	2 tbs.
salt	¾ tsp.	1¼ tsp.
Miller's bran	¾ cup	1 cup
bread flour	1¾ cups	2⅓ cups
vital gluten, optional	2 tsp.	1 tbs.
active dry yeast	1½ tsp.	2½ tsp.

Add at raisin/nut beep, 5 minutes before end of kneading phase, or work into dough:

dried blueberries	⅝ cup	¾ cup

BLUEBERRY WHOLE WHEAT BAGELS

Add a few berries in with the mix to give the dough color; then add the remainder later.

	1 pound	**1½ pound**
water	¾ cup	1⅛ cups
vegetable oil	1 tbs.	1 tbs.
malt syrup or brown sugar	1 tbs.	2 tbs.
salt	¾ tsp.	1¼ tsp.
whole wheat flour	¾ cup	1 cup
bread flour	1¾ cups	2⅓ cups
vital gluten, optional	2 tsp.	1 tbs.
active dry yeast	1½ tsp.	2½ tsp.

Add at raisin/nut beep, 5 minutes before end of kneading phase, or work into dough:

dried blueberries	½ cup	¾ cup

VARIATION: CHERRY BLUEBERRY BAGELS

Use a combination of dried cherries and blueberries, or any other dried berry available, in two or more combinations, in the same amounts as above.

CINNAMON RAISIN MULTIGRAIN BAGELS

Multigrain cereal contains seven (sometimes nine) different kinds of grains. It's easier to use one prepared multigrain product than trying to combine different kinds of whole grains in small amounts. This is a healthy, dense bagel.

	1 pound	**1½ pound**
water	¾ cup	1¼ cups
vegetable oil	1 tbs.	2 tbs.
brown sugar	1 tbs.	2 tbs.
salt	¾ tsp.	1 tsp.
cinnamon	1½ tsp.	1 tbs.
multigrain cereal	½ cup	1 cup
whole wheat flour	¼ cup	½ cup
bread flour	2 cups	2 cups
vital gluten, optional	2 tsp.	1 tbs.
active dry yeast	1½ tsp.	2½ tsp.

Add at raisin/nut beep, 5 minutes before end of kneading phase, or work into dough:

	1 pound	1½ pound
raisins	½ cup	¾ cup

CRANBERRY RAISIN BAGELS

This popular combination outsells all others at one of our local bagel shops. It has a pretty pink shiny crust and pinkish dough.

	1 pound	**1½ pound**
water	¾ cup	1⅛ cups
vegetable oil	1 tbs.	1 tbs.
malt syrup, molasses or honey	1 tbs.	2 tbs.
salt	¾ tsp.	1 tsp.
bread flour	2¾ cups	3⅓ cups
active dry yeast	1½ tsp.	2 tsp.

Add at raisin/nut beep, 5 minutes before end of kneading phase, or work into dough:

	1 pound	**1½ pound**
golden raisins	¼ cup	¼ cup
dried cranberries	¼ cup	½ cup

DATE NUT BAGELS

Dates and nuts are a favorite combination in quick breads and muffins. They are equally good in bagels. Try these with sunflower kernels instead of nuts, too.

	1 pound	**1½ pound**
water	¾ cup	1⅛ cups
vegetable oil	1 tbs.	1 tbs.
malt syrup or white sugar	1 tbs.	2 tbs.
salt	¾ tsp.	1 tsp.
bread flour	2¾ cups	3⅓ cups
active dry yeast	1½ tsp.	2 tsp.

Add at raisin/nut beep, 5 minutes before end of kneading phase, or work into dough:

	1 pound	**1½ pound**
nuts, finely chopped	½ cup	¾ cup
dates, chopped	⅝ cup	¾ cup

APRICOT BAGELS

You'll enjoy the sweet flavor and lovely color that apricots impart to the dough.

	1 pound	**1½ pound**
water	¾ cup	1⅛ cups
orange extract, optional	1 tsp.	2 tsp.
vegetable oil	1 tbs.	1 tbs.
honey, malt syrup or white sugar	1 tbs.	2 tbs.
salt	¾ tsp.	1 tsp.
bread flour	2¾ cups	3⅓ cups
active dry yeast	1½ tsp.	2 tsp.

Add at raisin/nut beep, 5 minutes before end of kneading phase, or work into dough:

dried apricots, diced	½ cup	¾ cup

VARIATION: PEACH BAGELS

Substitute peaches for the apricots.

dried peaches, diced	½ cup	¾ cup

HAWAIIAN BAGELS

Dried pineapple alone or combined with coconut is a unique combination. If available, use part coconut milk for liquid. If not, use all water in the same amount and add 1 tsp. coconut extract.

	1 pound	1½ pound
water	¼ cup	½ cup
coconut milk	½ cup	⅝ cup
or coconut extract	1 tsp.	1 tsp.
liquid should equal	*¾ cup*	*1⅛ cups*
malt syrup or white sugar	1 tbs.	2 tbs.
vegetable oil	1 tbs.	1 tbs.
salt	¾ tsp.	1 tsp.
bread flour	2¾ cups	3⅓ cups
active dry yeast	1½ tsp.	2 tsp.

Add at raisin/nut beep, 5 minutes before end of kneading phase, or work into dough:

dried pineapple, cut into pea-sized pieces	⅜ cup	½ cup
dried coconut, shredded or flaked	½ cup	⅝ cup

MARBLED CINNAMON-NUTMEG RYE BAGELS

Use a glaze and no topping so marbled effect of these delicious bagels is evident.

	1 pound	**1½ pound**
water	¾ cup	1⅛ cups
vegetable oil	1 tbs.	2 tbs.
honey	1 tbs.	2 tbs.
salt	¾ tsp.	1 tsp.
cocoa	½ tsp.	½ tsp.
caraway seeds	¼ cup	⅔ cup
cornmeal	¼ cup	⅓ cup
light rye flour	½ cup	¾ cup
bread flour	1¾ cups	2¼ cups
vital gluten, optional	2 tsp.	4 tsp.
active dry yeast	1½ tsp.	2½ tsp.

For marbled effect, combine and knead lightly into dough just before shaping:

cinnamon	1 tsp.	1 tbs.
nutmeg	½ tsp.	1 tsp.

PEANUT BUTTER CHIP BAGELS

Children eat these so quickly, you should plan on making one batch and refrigerating it while mixing a second, and then save time by boiling and baking both batches at once.

	1 pound	**1½ pound**
water	¾ cup	1⅛ cups
peanut butter, smooth or crunchy	1 tbs.	1½ tbs.
malt syrup or white sugar	1 tbs.	2 tbs.
salt	¾ tsp.	1 tsp.
bread flour	2¾ cups	3⅓ cups
active dry yeast	1½ tsp.	2 tsp.

Add at raisin/nut beep, 5 minutes before end of kneading phase, or work into dough:

peanut butter chips	½ cup	¾ cup

VARIATION: PEANUT BUTTER CHOCOLATE CHIP BAGELS

Use chocolate chips instead of, or combined with, peanut butter chips.

PEANUT HONEY CURRANT BAGELS

Chopped peanuts give these bagels crunch as well as peanut taste.

	1 pound	**1½ pound**
water	¾ cup	1⅛ cups
peanut butter, smooth or crunchy	1 tbs.	1½ tbs.
honey	1 tbs.	2 tbs.
salt	¾ tsp.	1 tsp.
bread flour	2¾ cups	3⅓ cups
active dry yeast	1½ tsp.	2 tsp.

Add at raisin/nut beep, 5 minutes before end of kneading phase, or work into dough:

peanuts, coarsely chopped	½ cup	⅝ cup
dried currants	¼ cup	⅜ cup

MIXED NUT BAGELS

Chop any variety of nuts together: pecans, walnuts, almonds, peanuts or others. Most machines will pulverize the nuts if you put them in at the beginning. You may want to add some at the raisin/nut beep and work in larger pieces of nuts, even quarters and halves, before you shape the dough, for great taste and texture.

	1 pound	**1½ pound**
water	¾ cup	1⅛ cups
vegetable oil	1 tbs.	1 tbs.
malt syrup or brown sugar	1 tbs.	2 tbs.
salt	¾ tsp.	1¼ tsp.
whole wheat flour	¾ cup	1 cup
bread flour	1¾ cups	2⅓ cups
vital gluten, optional	2 tsp.	1 tbs.
active dry yeast	1½ tsp.	2½ tsp.

Add at raisin/nut beep, 5 minutes before end of kneading phase, or work into dough:

mixed nuts, chopped	⅝ cup	¾ cup

CHOCOLATE CHIP BAGELS

Sounds like an unlikely combination, but it's absolutely delicious. For some reason when the chips are added in the machine, the dough doesn't rise as high. I noticed this in commercially made chocolate chip bagels as well as mine.

	1 pound	**1½ pound**
water	¾ cup	1⅛ cups
vegetable oil	1 tbs.	1 tbs.
malt syrup or brown sugar	1 tbs.	2 tbs.
salt	¾ tsp.	1 tsp.
cocoa powder	1 tbs.	2 tbs.
bread flour	2¾ cups	3⅓ cups
active dry yeast	1½ tsp.	2 tsp.

Add at raisin/nut beep, 5 minutes before end of kneading phase, or work into dough:

	1 pound	**1½ pound**
chocolate chips or mini chocolate chips	½ cup	¾ cup

VARIATION: RAISIN CHOCOLATE CHIP BAGELS

Add ¼ cup raisins or dried currants with the chocolate chips for either size recipe.

VEGETABLE BAGELS

GREEN CHILI BAGELS

Chili lovers unite! This New Mexico favorite is spreading across the country. Use canned diced green chilies, drained and patted dry on paper towels. Use half the amount of chilies at the beginning with the liquid ingredients, and the other half at the raisin/nut beep.

	1 pound	**1½ pound**
water	½ cup	⅞ cup
vegetable oil	1 tbs.	1 tbs.
malt syrup, molasses or white sugar	1 tbs.	2 tbs.
canned green chilies, drained	¼ cup	⅜ cup
salt	¾ tsp.	1 tsp.
chili powder	¼ tsp.	¼ tsp.
bread flour	2¾ cups	3⅓ cups
active dry yeast	1½ tsp.	2 tsp.

Add at raisin/nut beep or 5 minutes before end of kneading phase, or work into dough:

canned green chilies, drained	¼ cup	¼ cup

DILL-GREEN ONION BAGELS

Work extra dill and onions into the dough for texture just before shaping. If you don't have fresh dill, use dried dill and cut the amount to one-third.

	1 pound	**1½ pound**
water	¾ cup	1⅛ cups
vegetable or olive oil	1 tbs.	1 tbs.
malt syrup, molasses or white sugar	1 tbs.	2 tbs.
dill, chopped fresh	1 tbs.	1½ tbs.
green onions, minced	1 tbs.	2½ tbs.
salt	¾ tsp.	1 tsp.
bread flour	2¾ cups	3⅓ cups
active dry yeast	1½ tsp.	2 tsp.

Add at raisin/nut beep, 5 minutes before end of kneading phase, or work into dough:

dill, chopped fresh	2 tbs.	2 tbs.
green onions, minced	1½ tbs.	1½ tbs.

GARLIC BAGELS

If there were an indigenous Greek bagel, this would probably be the choice. Garlic-flavored olive oil would be the crowning ingredient, but any olive oil will yield excellent results. Sprinkle bagel tops with garlic salt before baking.

	1 pound	**1½ pound**
water	¾ cup	1⅛ cups
olive oil	3 tbs.	¼ cup
garlic cloves, peeled and lightly crushed	2 tsp.	2 tsp.
malt syrup or white sugar	1 tbs.	2 tbs.
salt	¾ tsp.	1¼ tsp.
bread flour	2¾ cups	3⅓ cups
active dry yeast	1½ tsp.	2 tsp.

Topping: **garlic salt**

JALAPEÑO CHEDDAR BAGELS

Jalapeño peppers are available in jars or cans in many supermarkets, delis and specialty food stores. Slice wet peppers in half, remove seeds and stems, chop and blot dry on a paper towel. These spicy bagels are wonderful in a mini size to serve with cocktails or as appetizers.

	1 pound	**1½ pound**
water	¾ cup	1⅛ cups
vegetable oil	1 tbs.	1 tbs.
malt syrup, molasses or white sugar	1 tbs.	2 tbs.
canned jalapeño peppers, drained, blotted, chopped	2 tbs.	3 tbs.
salt	¾ tsp.	1 tsp.
chili powder	¼ tsp.	¼ tsp.
cornmeal	¼ cup	¼ cup
whole wheat flour	½ cup	⅝ cup
bread flour	2 cups	2½ cups
active dry yeast	1½ tsp.	2 tsp.
Work into dough:		
mild cheddar cheese, shredded	⅓ cup	⅓ cup

SEEDED MULTIGRAIN BAGELS

Here's a healthy bagel that can serve as the basis for a health food sandwich. Slice and fill with tomatoes, lettuce and sprouts.

	1 pound	**1½ pound**
water	¾ cup	1⅛ cups
vegetable oil	1 tbs.	1 tbs.
malt syrup, honey or molasses	1 tbs.	2 tbs.
salt	¾ tsp.	1 tsp.
cornmeal	¼ cup	¼ cup
multigrain cereal	¾ cup	¾ cup
bread flour	1¾ cups	2⅓ cups
vital gluten, optional	2 tsp.	1 tbs.
active dry yeast	1½ tsp.	2½ tsp.

Add at raisin/nut beep, or 5 minutes before end of kneading phase:

sunflower seeds	¼ cup	½ cup
sesame seeds	¼ cup	¼ cup

Suggested toppings: **sesame seeds or poppy seeds**

OAT BRAN BAGELS WITH PUMPKIN SEEDS AND CINNAMON

This wonderful-tasting, popular combination can be made even more tempting by marbling with cinnamon. Work another teaspoon of cinnamon into dough before shaping. They're also delicious topped with sunflower or poppy seeds.

	1 pound	**1½ pound**
water	¾ cup	1⅛ cups
vegetable oil	1 tbs.	1 tbs.
malt syrup or molasses	1 tbs.	2 tbs.
salt	¾ tsp.	1 tsp.
cinnamon	1 tbs.	1½ tbs.
Miller's bran	⅛ cup	¼ cup
cornmeal	¼ cup	¼ cup
oats, uncooked (not instant)	½ cup	½ cup
bread flour	1½ cups	2½ cups
vital gluten, optional	2 tsp.	1 tbs.
active dry yeast	1½ tsp.	2½ tsp.

Add at raisin/nut beep, 5 minutes before end of kneading phase, or work into dough:

raw pumpkin seeds	½ cup	⅝ cup

ONION PEPPER RYE BAGELS

These used to be my father's favorite bagels, delivered warm to our back door on Sunday mornings. Red and green pepper flakes are made from sweet bell peppers, and can be found in health food stores. Use vegetable flakes if you can't find the pepper flakes.

	1 pound	1½ pound
water	⅞ cup	1⅓ cups
vegetable oil	1 tbs.	2 tbs.
malt syrup or molasses	2 tbs.	3 tbs.
salt	¾ tsp.	1 tsp.
caraway seeds	¼ cup	⅔ cup
red and green pepper flakes	¼ cup	¼ cup
onion powder	⅛ tsp.	½ tsp.
cornmeal	¼ cup	⅓ cup
light rye flour	½ cup	¾ cup
bread flour	2 cups	2⅓ cups
vital gluten, optional	2 tsp.	4 tsp.
active dry yeast	1½ tsp.	2½ tsp.

Suggested toppings: **caraway seeds or dried onion flakes**

ONION PUMPERNICKEL BAGELS

*Onions with rye and whole wheat have an entirely different flavor than onions in a rye dough only. Top bagels with onions, or combine salt, onion flakes, garlic flakes and seeds to make the **"Everything" Bagel**, a mainstay in many bagel bakeries.*

	1 pound	**1½ pound**
water	¾ cup	1⅛ cups
vegetable oil	1 tbs.	1 tbs.
malt syrup or honey	1 tbs.	2 tbs.
salt	¾ tsp.	1¼ tsp.
dried onion flakes	1 tbs.	1½ tbs.
instant coffee crystals or unsweetened cocoa powder	¾ tbs.	1 tbs.
rye flour	¼ cup	½ cup
whole wheat flour	¾ cup	1 cup
bread flour	1½ cups	2 cups
vital gluten, optional	2 tsp.	1 tbs.
active dry yeast	1½ tsp.	2½ tsp.

VARIATION: "EVERYTHING" BAGELS

Coarse salt or kosher salt, onion flakes, garlic flakes and seeds are mixed to top a whole wheat or white bagel.

PUMPKIN ORANGE BAGELS

A subtle orange color tints the basic white bagel.

	1 pound	1½ pound
orange juice	½ cup	⅝ cup
pumpkin puree	⅓ cup	½ cup
malt syrup, molasses or brown sugar	1 tbs.	2 tbs.
salt	¾ tsp.	1 tsp.
grated orange peel	½ tsp.	¾ tsp.
pumpkin pie spice	1½ tsp.	2 tsp.
cinnamon	¼ tsp.	¼ tsp.
bread flour	2¾ cups	3⅓ cups
active dry yeast	1½ tsp.	2 tsp.

WHOLE WHEAT BAGELS WITH ROSEMARY AND GREEN OLIVES

Sliced green olives, carefully folded into the dough, add interesting shapes and color to the bagel and combine with the rosemary for a piquant taste.

	1 pound	**1½ pound**
water	¾ cup	1⅛ cups
malt syrup or brown sugar	1 tbs.	2 tbs.
salt	¾ tsp.	1¼ tsp.
rosemary, dried	½ tsp.	¾ tsp.
whole wheat flour	¾ cup	1 cup
bread flour	2 cups	2⅓ cups
vital gluten, optional	2 tsp.	1 tbs.
active dry yeast	1½ tsp.	2½ tsp.

Add at raisin/nut beep, 5 minutes before end of kneading phase, or work into dough:

green olives, drained, sliced	¼ cup	½ cup

SUN-DRIED TOMATO AND BLACK OLIVE BAGELS

Sun-dried tomatoes are a delicacy of recent vintage. Find them where dried foods and speciality foods are sold. Sliver them to add to the machine, and then add rings of sliced black olives while hand-kneading for a delicious combination with eye appeal.

	1 pound	**1½ pound**
water	¾ cup	1⅛ cups
vegetable oil	1 tbs.	1 tbs.
malt syrup, molasses or brown sugar	1 tbs.	2 tbs.
salt	¾ tsp.	1 tsp.
cornmeal	¼ cup	½ cup
whole wheat flour	½ cup	¾ cup
bread flour	2 cups	2 cups
vital gluten, optional	2 tsp.	1 tbs.
active dry yeast	1½ tsp.	2½ tsp.

Add at raisin/nut beep or 5 minutes before end of kneading phase:

sun-dried tomatoes, slivered	⅜ cup	½ cup

Work into dough:

black olives, drained, sliced	⅜ cup	⅝ cup

VEGETABLE MEDLEY BAGELS

Red pepper, parsley, celery, onion, sun-dried tomatoes and chopped green or sliced black olives provide a flavor medley. Bagel bakers tell me they can't keep enough of these in their bins.

	1 pound	1½ pound
water	¾ cup	1⅛ cups
vegetable oil	1 tbs.	1 tbs.
malt syrup, molasses or brown sugar	1 tbs.	2 tbs.
mixed dried vegetables flakes	¼ cup	⅜ cup
salt	¾ tsp.	1 tsp.
cornmeal	¼ cup	½ cup
whole wheat flour	½ cup	¾ cup
bread flour	2 cups	2½ cups
vital gluten, optional	2 tsp.	1 tbs.
active dry yeast	1½ tsp.	2½ tsp.

Add at raisin/nut beep, 5 minutes before end of kneading phase, or work into dough:

green or black olives, drained, sliced	¼ cup	⅜ cup

HOLIDAY BAGELS

CHRISTMAS BAGELS

You can make bagels to eat, but they'll look good on a Christmas tree, too. Bake a batch of mini bagels, and attach them to your tree with plaid ribbon. For edible Christmas bagels, knead in red and green dried cherries. Add a drop of red food coloring to the liquid for a tinted dough, or knead in a few drops of color for a marbleized effect when you add red and green dried cherries.

	1 pound	**1½ pound**
water	¾ cup	1⅛ cups
red or green food coloring	6 drops	6 drops
vegetable oil	1 tbs.	1 tbs.
malt syrup, molasses or white sugar	1 tbs.	2 tbs.
salt	¾ tsp.	1 tsp.
bread flour	2¾ cups	3⅓ cups
active dry yeast	1½ tsp.	2 tsp.

Add at raisin/nut beep, 5 minutes before end of kneading phase, or work into dough:

red and green dried cherries, diced	½ cup	½ cup

EASTER EGG BAGELS WITH CANDY SPRINKLES

A basic egg bagel recipe represents the tradition of an Easter egg. But hand-knead colorful candy sprinkles or other sugar nonpareils into the dough and they will leave trails of color in the finished bread. Add some for topping, too.

	1 pound	**1½ pound**
water	⅝ cup	⅞ cup
medium egg	1	1
vegetable oil	1 tbs.	1 tbs.
brown sugar	1½ tbs.	2 tbs.
salt	¾ tsp.	1 tsp.
bread flour	2¾ cups	3⅓ cups
active dry yeast	1½ tsp.	2 tsp.

Work into dough:

multicolored candy sprinkles	⅓ cup	½ cup

Bake in a 350° oven for about 20 minutes or until golden brown.

EASTER EGG BAGELS - NO BOILING

Here's a variation of the egg bagel that requires no boiling. The result is a soft, tasty bagel that will save time on a busy holiday. Serve it with your Easter dinner or use it for leftover ham sandwiches.

	1 pound	**1½ pound**
water	½ cup	¾ cup
large egg	1	1
butter or margarine	2 tbs.	3 tbs.
sugar	1½ tbs.	2 tbs.
salt	1 tsp.	1½ tsp.
bread flour	2¾ cups	3⅓ cups
dry milk	2 tbs.	3 tbs.
active dry yeast	1½ tsp.	1¾ tsp.

Glaze: 1 egg beaten with 1 tbs. water

Suggested toppings: coarse salt, sesame seeds, poppy seeds, reconstituted dried onion flakes

Upon completion of the dough cycle, shape bagels and allow a second rise for 20 to 30 minutes or until about doubled in size. DO NOT BOIL. Brush with glaze, sprinkle with topping and bake in a preheated 350° oven for 10 to 15 minutes or until golden brown.

FOURTH OF JULY BAGELS

A bagel loaded with dried red cherries, dried blueberries and white chocolate chips is the perfect red, white and blue color combination for Independence Day. Use this recipe for Flag Day, too. For variety, add 6 drops blue food coloring to the liquid, and omit blueberries.

	1 pound	**1½ pound**
water	¾ cup	1⅛ cups
vegetable oil	1 tbs.	1 tbs.
malt syrup or white sugar	1 tbs.	2 tbs.
salt	¾ tsp.	1 tsp.
cornmeal	⅓ cup	⅓ cup
whole wheat flour	¼ cup	¾ cup
bread flour	2¼ cups	2¼ cups
vital gluten, optional	1 tsp.	1 tbs.
active dry yeast	1½ tsp.	2½ tsp.

Add at raisin/nut beep, 5 minutes before end of kneading phase, or work into dough:

dried cherries	¼ cup	¼ cup
dried blueberries	¼ cup	¼ cup
white chocolate chips	¼ cup	¼ cup

HALLOWEEN PAPAYA AND LICORICE BAGELS

Find unusual ingredients that can add symbolic color to a bagel so they're extra eye-appealing and tasty. Diced pieces of dried papaya and thin slices of black licorice are a taste and color surprise.

	1 pound	**1½ pound**
water	¾ cup	1⅛ cups
vegetable oil	1 tbs.	1 tbs.
malt syrup or brown sugar	1 tbs.	2 tbs.
salt	¾ tsp.	1 tsp.
cornmeal	⅛ cup	⅛ cup
whole wheat flour	¼ cup	½ cup
bread flour	2½ cups	2¾ cups
vital gluten, optional	1 tsp.	1 tbs.
active dry yeast	1½ tsp.	2½ tsp.

Add at raisin/nut beep, 5 minutes before end of kneading phase, or work into dough:

dried papaya, cut into pea-sized pieces	¼ cup	⅜ cup
black licorice twists, thinly sliced	¼ cup	⅜ cup

HALLOWEEN PUMPKIN BAGELS

What would Halloween be without pumpkins? What would Halloween bagels be without a pumpkin flavor? Use pureed cooked fresh pumpkin or canned pumpkin. The bagel will have a soft orange tint.

	1 pound	**1½ pound**
water	½ cup	⅝ cup
pumpkin puree	⅓ cup	½ cup
malt syrup, molasses or brown sugar	1 tbs.	2 tbs.
salt	¾ tsp.	1 tsp.
pumpkin pie spice	1½ tsp.	2 tsp.
cinnamon	1 tsp.	1½ tsp.
bread flour	2¾ cups	3⅓ cups
active dry yeast	1½ tsp.	2 tsp.

Add at raisin/nut beep, 5 minutes before end of kneading phase, or work into dough:

pumpkin seeds	⅓ cup	½ cup

ST. PATRICK'S DAY BAGELS

Color dough green, add bits of dried green cherries and perhaps the Irish will trade shamrocks for bagels. If the dough is not green enough at the raisin/nut beep, add a few more drops of coloring.

	1 pound	**1½ pound**
water	¾ cup	1⅛ cups
green food coloring	6 drops	6-8 drops
vegetable oil	1 tbs.	1 tbs.
molasses, honey or white sugar	1 tbs.	2 tbs.
salt	¾ tsp.	1 tsp.
bread flour	2¾ cups	3⅓ cups
active dry yeast	1½ tsp.	2 tsp.

Add at raisin/nut beep, 5 minutes before end of kneading phase, or work into dough:

dried green cherries, quartered	½ cup	¾ cup

THANKSGIVING BAGELS WITH PUMPKIN, APPLES AND NUTS

Get a head start on your Thanksgiving dinner by serving your guests these delicious bagels for breakfast. They're good for turkey sandwiches, too.

	1 pound	**1½ pound**
water	½ cup	⅝ cup
pumpkin puree	⅓ cup	½ cup
vegetable oil	1 tbs.	1 tbs.
malt syrup, molasses or brown sugar	1 tbs.	2 tbs.
salt	¾ tsp.	1 tsp.
pumpkin pie spice	1½ tsp.	2 tsp.
bread flour	2¾ cups	3⅓ cups
active dry yeast	1½ tsp.	2 tsp.

Add at raisin/nut beep, 5 minutes before end of kneading phase, or work into dough:

dried apples, diced	⅓ cup	½ cup
walnuts, chopped	¼ cup	⅝ cup

THANKSGIVING BAGELS WITH SWEET POTATOES AND FRUIT

Here's a nourishing bread that will also use up leftover sweet potatoes advantageously. It makes a high-rising, subtle-tasting bagel.

	1 pound	**1½ pound**
water	⅝ cup	1 cup
orange extract	1½ tsp.	1½ tsp.
cooked sweet potatoes, sliced or mashed	⅓ cup	½ cup
malt syrup, molasses or brown sugar	1 tbs.	2 tbs.
salt	¾ tsp.	1 tsp.
whole wheat flour	½ cup	⅝ cup
bread flour	2¼ cups	2¾ cups
vital gluten, optional	1 tsp.	1 tbs.
active dry yeast	1½ tsp.	2½ tsp.

Add at raisin/nut beep, 5 minutes before end of kneading phase, or work into dough:

dried mixed fruits, diced	⅓ cup	½ cup

ORANGE-CRANBERRY THANKSGIVING BAGELS

With these special bagels on the table, there will be lots more to be thankful for at this wonderful time of family gatherings and feasting.

	1 pound	**1½ pound**
water	¼ cup	⅝ cup
orange juice	½ cup	½ cup
grated orange peel	1½ tbs.	2 tbs.
brown sugar or molasses	1 tbs.	2 tbs.
salt	¾ tsp.	1 tsp.
bread flour	2¾ cups	3⅓ cups
active dry yeast	1½ tsp.	2 tsp.

Add at raisin/nut beep, 5 minutes before end of kneading phase, or work into dough:

dried cranberries	½ cup	¾ cup

VALENTINE'S DAY BERRY BAGELS

Red berry-flavored bagels are one way to win anyone's heart. Use dried strawberries, raspberries or cherries. Work a few drops of red food coloring into the dough before you shape it to add a soft pink marbelized color. Put 1/3 cup red heart candies in your food processor, chop coarsely and sprinkle on for topping.

	1 pound	**1½ pound**
water	¾ cup	1⅛ cups
vegetable oil	1 tbs.	1 tbs.
honey or white sugar	1 tbs.	2 tbs.
salt	¾ tsp.	1 tsp.
whole wheat flour	¾ cup	¾ cup
bread flour	2 cups	2¾ cups
vital gluten, optional	1 tsp.	1 tbs.
active dry yeast	1½ tsp.	2½ tsp.

Add at raisin/nut beep, 5 minutes before end of kneading phase, or work into dough:

red food coloring	6 drops	6 drops
dried strawberries, raspberries or cherries	½ cup	¾ cup

Suggested topping: **coarsely chopped red heart candies**

WASHINGTON'S BIRTHDAY CHERRY BAGELS

If early Americans had known about cherry bagels, they might have become more popular than cherry pie. George Washington would have cut down the cherry tree for a mighty good reason. Use dried cherries and hand-knead into dough. If coloring is not strong enough, add a few more drops to dough during kneading phase.

	1 pound	**1½ pound**
water	¾ cup	1⅛ cups
red food coloring	6 drops	6 drops
honey, molasses or white sugar	1 tbs.	2 tbs.
vegetable oil	1 tbs.	1 tbs.
salt	¾ tsp.	1 tsp.
bread flour	2¾ cups	3⅓ cups
active dry yeast	1½ tsp.	2 tsp.

Work into dough:

dried cherries, chopped	½ cup	¾ cup

HANUKKAH CHOCOLATE CHIP AND CANDY BAGELS

Children love Hanukkah, which falls during December and lasts for eight glorious food-and-fun-filled days. It's gift-giving time, as each night's candle lighting of a special menorah symbolizes the ancient temple, where only a small vial of oil miraculously kept the menorah lit for eight days and nights. Make special bagels using jelly for sweetening, and add chocolate chips and colorful nonpareil candies.

	1 pound	**1½ pound**
water	¾ cup	1⅛ cups
vegetable oil	1 tbs.	1 tbs.
strawberry jelly	½ tbs.	1 tbs.
white sugar	¾ tbs.	1 tbs.
salt	¾ tsp.	1 tsp.
multicolored candy sprinkles	½ cup	½ cup
bread flour	2¾ cups	3⅓ cups
active dry yeast	1½ tsp.	2½ tsp.

Add at raisin/nut beep, 5 minutes before end of kneading phase, or work into dough:

chocolate chips	⅜ cup	½ cup
candy sprinkles	¼ cup	¼ cup

Suggested topping: **additional candy sprinkles**

PURIM BAGELS

The Jewish holiday of Purim is a festive time for a joyous celebration of an ancient event, when Jews foiled wicked Haman's plot to put their beloved Queen Esther to death. Foods of this holiday vary in different countries. The most popular food is hamantaschen (taken from the name "Haman"). It's a triangular-shaped bread that represents Haman's hat, or ears, or nose, depending on whose version you're reading, and it is usually filled with poppy seed, apricot, raisin or other filling. This is my revised version. Top with poppy seeds before baking.

	1 pound	**1½ pound**
water	¾ cup	1⅛ cups
vegetable oil	1 tbs.	1 tbs.
honey, malt syrup or white sugar	1 tbs.	2 tbs.
salt	¾ tsp.	1 tsp.
poppy seeds	¼ cup	⅜ cup
bread flour	2¾ cups	3⅓ cups
active dry yeast	1½ tsp.	2 tsp.

Add at raisin/nut beep, 5 minutes before end of kneading phase, or work into dough:

	1 pound	**1½ pound**
raisins	⅓ cup	½ cup

PASSOVER MATZO BAGELS WITH HONEY GLAZE

Passover breads must be "unleavened" or made without yeast. They won't taste like yeast bagels, but they are so incredibly delicious you may want to make them all year around. Don't make these in your bread machine. Use a food processor, electric mixer or an egg beater. This recipe makes about 14 bagels.

½ cup vegetable oil
1½ cups water
1 tsp. salt
1 tsp. sugar

2½ cups matzo meal
4 eggs
Honey Glaze, follows
chopped nuts for topping

Place oil, water, salt and sugar in a 1½-quart saucepan and bring to a full rolling boil. Remove from heat. Add matzo meal all at once; beat until smooth and well blended. Add eggs, 1 at a time, beating well after each addition until mixture is smooth and well blended. Coat hands with oil; break off pieces of dough about the size of an egg. Shape into bagels, place on a well-greased baking sheet and bake in a preheated 350° oven for 50 to 60 minutes. About 15 minutes before end of baking time, spoon glaze over each bagel. Remove bagels from oven when done and sprinkle with chopped nuts.

HONEY GLAZE

½ cup water
¼ cup honey
½ cup sugar
¼ tsp. cinnamon
2 tbs. vegetable oil or margarine
½ cup finely chopped nuts

Combine water, honey, sugar and cinnamon in a small saucepan and bring to a boil over medium heat. Boil for 2 minutes, stirring constantly. Add oil or margarine. Cool.

ROSH HASHANAH APPLE-HONEY BAGELS

Rosh Hashanah is the Jewish New Year, a High Holy Day filled with happiness and families gathering to wish one another health and fortune. It's a time for feasting and using sweet foods to symbolize a "sweet year" to come. Rosh Hashanah is always in September or October, when apples and dates are harvested, and there is ample honey from bees. So why not use them in bagels that will start breakfasts and days of the New Year off right?

	1 pound	1½ pound
water	½ cup	¾ cup
applesauce	¼ cup	⅜ cup
honey	1 tbs.	2 tbs.
salt	¾ tsp.	1 tsp.
bread flour	2¾ cups	3⅓ cups
active dry yeast	1½ tsp.	2 tsp.

Add at raisin/nut beep, 5 minutes before end of kneading phase, or work into dough:

dried apples, diced	½ cup	¾ cup

Work into dough:

dates, chopped	¼ cup	½ cup

Suggested toppings: **poppy seeds, sesame seeds, chopped nuts**

SABBATH SOFT CARROT BAGELS - NO BOILING

These bagels are quick to make because they omit the boiling step. A change of pace from chewy grain bagels, these are good for breakfast and a perfect accompaniment to other meals as well. Try them in mini sizes, 12 to 14 from the larger recipe.

	1 pound	1½ pound
water	½ cup	¾ cup
carrot, peeled, grated	⅜ cup	1⅛ cups
egg (or 2 egg whites)	1	1
vegetable oil	1½ tbs.	2 tbs.
sugar	1 tbs.	2 tbs.
salt	¾ tsp.	1 tsp.
anise seeds	½ tsp.	¾ tsp.
whole wheat flour	¼ cup	½ cup
bread flour or unbleached flour	2¼ cups	3¼ cups
vital gluten, optional	2 tsp.	1 tbs.
active dry yeast	1½ tsp.	2½ tsp.

Glaze, optional: **spray with water**
Suggested topping: **poppy seeds**

After the second rise, DO NOT BOIL. Bake in a 350° oven for about 20 minutes or until golden brown.

SHAVUOTH HARVEST TIME BAGELS

Shavuoth marks the receiving of the Ten Commandments on Mount Sinai and it is also the time of spring harvest. Harvested seeds and those used for planting new crops are part of the festival and make a delicious bagel for this special occasion.

	1 pound	**1½ pound**
water	¾ cup	1⅛ cups
vegetable oil	1 tbs.	1 tbs.
molasses or brown sugar	1 tbs.	2 tbs.
salt	¾ tsp.	1¼ tsp.
cornmeal	¼ cup	¼ cup
multigrain cereal	½ cup	½ cup
whole wheat flour	½ cup	¾ cup
bread flour	1½ cups	2¼ cups
vital gluten, optional	2 tsp.	1 tbs.
active dry yeast	1½ tsp.	2½ tsp.

Combine the following and add ¼ of mixture at raisin/nut beep or 5 minutes before end of kneading phase; use remainder for topping.

sunflower seeds	¼ cup	⅜ cup
sesame seeds	⅛ cup	¼ cup
poppy seeds	⅛ cup	¼ cup
celery seeds	2 tbs.	2 tbs.

SUCCOTH CORN-RYE BAGELS

Succoth is harvest time and comparable to Thanksgiving. Corn is an integral part of the harvest, and this bagel is a perfect complement to the holiday.

	1 pound	1½ pound
water	¾ cup	1 cup
almond extract	1 tsp.	1½ tsp.
vanilla extract	1 tsp.	1½ tsp.
vegetable oil	2 tsp.	1 tbs.
malt syrup or molasses	1 tbs.	2 tbs.
salt	⅔ tsp.	¾ tsp.
grated orange peel	1 tbs.	1 tbs.
cinnamon	2 tsp.	2½ tsp.
cornmeal, white or yellow	⅓ cup	⅓ cup
whole wheat flour	1 cup	1⅓ cups
bread flour	1½ cups	2½ cups
vital gluten, optional	2 tsp.	1 tbs.
active dry yeast	2 tsp.	2½ tsp.
Top with:		
almonds, coarsely chopped	½ cup	½ cup

BREAK-THE-FAST ORANGE-HONEY MINI BAGELS

Yom Kippur, the Day of Atonement, is the holiest of Holy Days in the Jewish calendar. It occurs ten days after Rosh Hashanah, but instead of celebrating, it's a time for atoning and repenting for one's sins. This day is set aside for prayer and a 24-hour fast. The fast is broken with a light meal, and bagels and cream cheese are often as much a tradition of the evening as the holiday itself. Bake mini bagels lightly flavored with honey and marbled with cinnamon and nutmeg. Serve them with a dish of honey for dipping.

	1 pound	**1½ pound**
water	¾ cup	1⅛ cups
vegetable oil	1 tbs.	2 tbs.
sugar	1 tbs.	1 tbs.
orange honey	1 tbs.	2 tbs.
salt	¾ tsp.	1 tsp.
bread flour	2¾ cups	3⅓ cups
active dry yeast	1½ tsp.	2 tsp.
Work into dough:		
cinnamon	1 tbs.	1½ tbs.
nutmeg	¾ tbs.	1 tbs.

SPREADS FOR BAGELS

Associating bagels with cream cheese is as natural as thinking of moms and apple pie. Of course, there's nothing wrong with unaltered cream cheese, but combine it creatively with herbs, spices, fruits, vegetables, jellies and jams, and the good tastes multiply.

ALL CREAM CHEESES ARE NOT THE SAME

Think cream cheese and probably the first image you conjure is a silver paper-wrapped package of PHILADELPHIA BRAND Cream Cheese in perfectly shaped 3- or 8-ounce bricks. Today, there are different types of cream cheeses packaged by a variety of companies — "lite," "fat-free," "whipped" and "soft" varieties. How are they alike and different?

Cream cheese is a soft, uncured cheese made of cow's milk, with cream added. The type was originated in 1872 by a dairyman from Chester, New York, named Lawrence. The special richness and smoothness of cream cheese comes from the whole milk and added cream. It is one of the few world-famous cheeses made by the lactic acid method rather than the rennet method of coagulating the curd. In 1880, another cheese maker contracted to distribute the cheese under the PHILADELPHIA BRAND trademark. In the late 19th century, Philadelphia was known for its superb-quality dairy products, so the cheese was named for Philadelphia although it was not made there. PHILADELPHIA BRAND Cream Cheese became a Kraft product in 1928.

Neufchatel cheese is a soft rennet cheese made of cow's milk. Its major source is the Department of Seine Inferieura, France. Neufchatel is made in the same manner as cream cheese, but its moisture content is higher, its fat content and calories are lower, and it is softer than the standard cream cheese. It is sometimes flavored with pimientos or spices.

Light cream cheese has one-third less fat than regular cream cheese. Generally skim milk replaces whole milk and reduces the fat content. Its name and fat content may vary by cheese-processing companies. Check labels among products and compare calorie and fat content.

Fat-free or nonfat cream cheese offers consumers zero fat content.

Soft cream cheese was introduced in 1980 under the PHILADELPHIA BRAND, and is now available under many different brands. It is nearly identical in flavor to brick cream cheese; however, the body and texture are significantly different. Also on the market are light and fat-free soft cream cheeses.

Whipped cream cheese has a fluffy consistency due to a whipping process that incorporates air into the cheese. Whipped cream cheese is available already flavored as well as plain.

STORING AND FREEZING CHEESES

Cream cheese and Neufchatel cheese are very perishable and should be refrigerated until ready to use. Kraft Food Company recommends that once opened, either rewrap or reseal the product in its original package and place it in an additional plastic storage bag or other airtight container. Refrigerate immediately and use within 2 weeks after opening.

Many cheese packages are dated with a "best when purchased by" caution. Look for the dates on a box top, an end flap, a package sleeve or the bottom of a tub.

Also in your grocer's refrigerators are cottage cheese, farmer's cheese, ricotta cheese, Dutch cheese and pot cheese. All are variations of a textured cheese made of pasteurized skim milk to which lactic acid cultures are added. Many can be substituted for cream cheese in the recipes given.

Refrigeration is the best storage for cheese. However, if you have more cheese than can be used before the freshness date stamped on the package, the following guidelines are suggested:

- Do not freeze cream cheese that you want to use for spreading, because there will be a texture change. Regular brick cream cheese can be frozen for up to 2 months for use as an ingredient in recipes. Thaw in the refrigerator for approximately 12 hours or overnight.
- Whipped cream cheese may be frozen for up to 6 months and still retain an acceptable quality for spreading.
- Soft cream cheese, light cream cheese, fat-free cream cheese and Neufchatel cheese should not be frozen.

SOFTENING AND SERVING CREAM CHEESE

Warm a brick of cheese to room temperature, cut it into chunks and mash it with a fork. Add up to 5 teaspoons of milk, cream, yogurt or other liquid, a little at a time, and whip with a food processor, blender, hand mixer, wire whisk or fork until smooth, creamy and of spreading consistency. Soft cream cheese and Neufchatel cheese are already of spreading consistency.

The following recipes are for 8-ounce packages of cheese and about 5 teaspoons of milk or other liquid ingredient.

For serving, plan on 1 ounce of cream cheese for topping each bagel half. An 8-ounce package of cream cheese, sliced into rectangles, will yield enough spread for 8 half-bagels, or about 4 servings.

Cream cheese is also available in a 3-pound brick, which is more economical than the 8-ounce size when preparing large quantities. Soften by cutting into smaller pieces and warm at room temperature for about an hour or set in the microwave on MEDIUM for 30 seconds or until softened. Use a commercial mixer, if available. Or blend small portions at a time with a food processor, mixer or blender.

If you're watching calories, substitute any of the lower calorie, low fat cheese products including nonfat yogurt, sour cream, ricotta cheese, or even applesauce or apple butter for regular cream cheese.

Cream cheese spreads flavored with fruits are as popular as bagels with fruits added. Serve the fruity spreads at breakfast, and for a snack any time of the day. Mix fruit with the cheese according to the recipes. Or spread your bagel with cream cheese, butter, jelly, jam or lemon curd and top with sliced or mashed fruit.

When spreads have been refrigerated to blend flavors, allow them to return to room temperature before serving, so they will be of spreading consistency.

LOX CREAM CHEESE SPREAD

Among bagel aficionados, lox and cream cheese is the classic combination that has catapulted bagels into a gourmet category. Still, many people are unfamiliar with it. There's a joke about the two Texans who wanted to try lox and bagels during their first trip to New York. When the dish arrived, they looked at it quizzically and asked, "Which is the lox and which is the bagel?" Lox is salmon cured in brine. Swedish gravlak includes dill. There is also Nova Scotia salmon, or Nova, a different salmon prepared with a cold-smoke method. See pages 149 and 150 for recipes.

6 thin slices lox, about 1/4 lb.
8 oz. cream cheese, softened
5 tsp. milk (or enough for spreading consistency)

Cut lox into about 1/2-inch squares. Combine with softened cream cheese and stir well with a wooden spoon. Add milk as needed. When large quantities are needed, combine softened cream cheese and lox with an electric mixer. Makes 4 to 6 servings.

SMOKED SALMON, SCOTCH AND CHIVES

Pumpernickel or rye bagels are excellent bases for this spread.

8 oz. cream cheese, softened
1/2 lb. smoked salmon
2 tbs. Scotch whisky
2 tsp. lemon juice

1/2 tsp. horseradish
dash cayenne pepper
2 tbs. chopped fresh chives or scallions

Place all ingredients except chives in a food processor bowl and process until well mixed. Add chives and pulse to mix. Store well covered in the refrigerator for up to 3 days. Makes 4 to 6 servings.

SMOKED SALMON MOUSSE

You can find this delicious product in plastic containers in delis and gourmet food shops, or make your own in your food processor.

8 oz. cream cheese, softened
4 slices cured salmon (lox, gravlak or Nova)
1 tsp. lemon juice

1 tsp. dried onion flakes
1/2 tsp. sugar
1/4 tsp. garlic powder
1/4 tsp. horseradish

Process all ingredients with a food processor until smooth. Makes 4 to 6 servings.

PICKLED HERRING WITH CREAM CHEESE

You'll find pickled herring in jars in your grocer's refrigerator cases.

1 jar (8 oz.) pickled herring with onions or herring in wine sauce
8 oz. cream cheese, softened
5 tsp. milk (or enough for spreading consistency)

Drain herring and remove bones. Chop herring plus onions from the jar. Blend with cream cheese and milk, and chill before serving. Or just spoon chopped herring on top of cream cheese brick and serve. Makes 4 to 6 servings.

SHRIMP SPREAD

This is perfect for a buffet brunch or a quick appetizer when friends drop by.

8 oz. cream cheese, in brick shape
½ cup cocktail sauce
1 can (4 oz.) shrimp, or 4 oz. chopped fresh shrimp

Place brick of cheese on a serving plate and cover with cocktail sauce. Top with shrimp. Serve with halved white mini bagels. Makes 4 to 6 servings.

BANANAS WITH CREAM CHEESE

Serve fruity spreads for breakfast, or for snacks anytime.

4 ripe bananas
1 tsp. lemon juice
8 oz. cream cheese, softened
5 tsp. milk (or enough for spreading consistency)

Mash bananas and mix with lemon juice to prevent browning. Combine softened cream cheese and banana. Add milk, a teaspoon at a time, and mix until cheese is of spreading consistency. Makes 8 to 10 servings.

CREAMY ORANGE SPREAD

Serve in a bowl surrounded by freshly baked bagel halves for a breakfast treat.

8 oz. cream cheese, softened
5 tsp. milk (or enough for spreading consistency)
1/4 cup orange marmalade

Combine ingredients. Makes 6 to 8 servings.

BLUEBERRY CHEESE SPREAD

Surround with a rim of whole fresh blueberries to serve.

⅓ cup fresh blueberries, or ¼ cup blueberry jelly
8 oz. cream cheese, softened
5 tsp. milk (or enough for spreading consistency)

Lightly mash blueberries with a fork before combining ingredients. Makes 6 to 8 servings.

CHEESY STRAWBERRY SPREAD

It's as delicious as strawberries on shortcake, but better for breakfasts and snacks when spread on a fresh, warm bagel.

8 oz. cream cheese, softened
5 tsp. milk (or enough for spreading consistency)
⅓ cup fresh strawberries, chopped, or ¼ cup strawberry jelly or jam, or
  ¼ cup frozen strawberries, thawed

Combine ingredients. Makes 6 to 8 servings.

CINNAMON-RAISIN SPREAD

Make plain bagels extraordinary with a little extra pizzazz.

8 oz. cream cheese, softened
1 tsp. cinnamon
1/3 cup coarsely chopped dark or golden raisins

Combine ingredients. Makes 6 to 8 servings.

JELLY AND CREAM CHEESE

This old standby combination pleases everyone.

8 oz. cream cheese, softened
5 tsp. milk (or enough for spreading consistency)
1/3 cup favorite jelly or jam

Combine ingredients. Makes 6 to 8 servings.

MAPLE-WALNUT SPREAD

This sweet, crunchy spread is wonderful as a dessert treat.

8 oz. cream cheese, softened
5 tsp. milk (or enough for spreading
    consistency)

1 tbs. maple sugar
½ cup finely ground walnuts

Combine ingredients. Makes 4 to 6 servings.

APPLE-CHEDDAR SPREAD

This makes a meal in a bagel for lunch or brunch. Serve with fruited bagels.

8 oz. cream cheese, softened
5 tsp. milk (or enough for spreading
    consistency)
1 cup (4 oz.) shredded mild cheddar
    cheese

¼ cup finely chopped apple
¼ cup finely chopped walnuts
½ tbs. sugar
¼ tsp. cinnamon
¼ tsp. nutmeg

Combine all ingredients with a mixer, a blender or a food processor until well blended. Makes 10 to 14 servings.

CHUTNEY AND CREAM CHEESE

Any flavored chutney by itself makes a wonderful spread for bagels, but layer it over cream cheese and it's an unusual piquant, sweet-sour combination that's sure to please the palates of discriminating bagel lovers. Chutney is a condiment of Indian origin made from a puree of seeded raisins, ginger, pimientos, mustard, brown sugar and vinegar with another fruit added. Apple, peach, pear, cranberry and mango chutney are so popular, they're now available in many supermarkets and specialty food stores. But chutneys can be made at home and canned or frozen. Here's a basic chutney recipe for canning that will yield about 8 half-pint jars.

PEAR CHUTNEY

10 cups sliced pears (about 5 lb.), skin,
  seeds and stems removed
1/2 cup finely chopped green bell pepper
1 1/2 cups raisins
4 cups sugar
1 cup chopped crystallized ginger

3 cups white vinegar
1/2 tsp. salt
1/2 tsp. ground cloves
1/2 tsp. allspice
3 three-inch cinnamon sticks

Combine pears, pepper, raisins, sugar, ginger, vinegar and salt in large kettle. Tie cloves, allspice and cinnamon sticks in a double-thickness square of cheesecloth and add to kettle. Bring mixture to a boil, stirring often. Reduce heat and simmer for 1 to 2 hours, stirring frequently, until chutney is dark and syrupy. Prepare fruit jars in normal canning procedure. Remove spice bag from mixture. Fill canning jars, cool and store. Yields 4 pints, or 20 to 30 servings.

VARIATIONS

PLUM CHUTNEY
Substitute 12 cups pitted, unpeeled, sliced blue plums for the pears.

PEACH CHUTNEY
Substitute 10 cups pitted, peeled, sliced peaches for the pears.

MANGO CHUTNEY
Substitute 10 cups pitted, peeled, diced mangoes for the pears. Or combine mangoes and papaya.

CRANBERRY CHUTNEY

Just as a combination of cranberry and raisins is tasty for bagels themselves, cranberry chutney is a delightful topping for plain bagels. It's easy to make. No preserving procedures are necessary because the recipe yields only 2½ cups, which are bound to disappear quickly.

1 cup water
1 cup sugar
1 pkg. (12 oz.) fresh or frozen
  cranberries
½ cup vinegar
1 cup raisins

½ cup peeled, diced apple
¼ tsp. allspice
¼ tsp. ground ginger
¼ tsp. cinnamon
⅛ tsp. ground cloves

Bring water and sugar to a boil in a medium saucepan over medium heat. Add remaining ingredients; return to a boil. Reduce heat and simmer for 15 minutes or until apples are tender. Pour into a glass mixing bowl.

Place a piece of plastic wrap directly on chutney. Cool to room temperature; then refrigerate overnight, covered with plastic wrap, so flavors blend. Serve at room temperature to use directly on bagels or over a layer of cream cheese. Yields 2½ cups, or 10 to 16 servings.

PLUM SAUCE AND CREAM CHEESE

A combination that most people would overlook is plum sauce and cream cheese. Plum sauce, often served with Chinese egg rolls, is available commercially, but you can create an excellent facsimile by mixing vinegar with plum or grape jelly.

½ cup plum or grape jelly
¼ cup white vinegar
8 oz. cream cheese

Combine jelly and vinegar and stir until well blended. Spread half a bagel with cream cheese, and then with sauce. Makes 6 to 8 servings.

MOCHA-ALMOND CINNAMON SPREAD

This spread is wonderful on chocolate chip or plain bagels.

8 oz. cream cheese, softened
5 tbs. brewed coffee (or enough for spreading consistency)
½ cup chopped toasted almonds or raw pine nuts
¼ tsp. cinnamon

Combine ingredients. Makes 6 to 8 servings.

SCALLION SPREAD

Green onions, or scallions, combine with cream cheese for a tasty topping.

8 oz. cream cheese, softened
5 tsp. milk (or enough for spreading consistency)
2-3 scallions, very finely chopped

Combine ingredients. Makes 4 to 6 servings.

CREAM CHEESE WITH SOY SAUCE

What could be easier when you want a quick appetizer? Perfect for mini bagels.

$\frac{1}{4}$ cup soy sauce
8 oz. cream cheese, in brick shape, softened
2 tbs. toasted sesame seeds

Pour soy sauce into a shallow dish and add brick of cheese. Turn cheese frequently until all sides are colored, about 10 minutes. Remove cheese from marinade, drain and place on a serving plate. Top with sesame seeds and serve with halved mini bagels. Makes 4 to 6 servings.

HOT BACON, CHEESE AND SCALLION TOPPING

Savory and delicious! If mayonnaise-cheese mixture does not blend easily, microwave on MEDIUM for 30 seconds until it attains spreading consistency.

1/2 cup mayonnaise
8 oz. cream cheese, softened
4 oz. sharp Monterey Jack cheese, shredded

2 tbs. very finely chopped scallions (green onions)
8 slices crisply fried bacon, cooled and crumbled

Mix mayonnaise and cheeses until well blended and smooth. Blend in onions and bacon crumbs. Spread on bagels and heat under the broiler until topping bubbles slightly. Do not burn. Makes 10 to 14 servings.

QUICK SOUTH-OF-THE-BORDER SPREAD

Green chilies are available in mild and hot varieties. Choose the taste you like.

8 oz. cream cheese or Neufchatel cheese, softened
1 can (4 oz.) chopped green chilies, drained
garlic salt

Combine cream cheese and chilies and blend well. Add garlic salt to taste. Chill. Makes 4 to 6 servings.

TOMATO CHEESE SPREAD

This spread is also good with the addition of Italian herbs, oregano or other favorite herbs that go well with tomatoes.

8 oz. cream cheese, softened
5 tsp. milk (or enough for spreading consistency)
3 tomatoes, seeded and chopped

Combine ingredients. Makes 8 to 10 servings.

CHEESE SPREAD WITH CAPERS AND ONIONS

Serve this favorite spread with a slice of tomato, or omit the scallions and add a slice of red onion with the tomato slice on each bagel half. Try it with light cream cheese, too.

8 oz. cream cheese, softened
5 tsp. milk (or enough for spreading consistency)
2-3 scallions, very finely chopped
2 tbs. drained capers

Combine ingredients. Makes 4 to 6 servings.

SALSA AND CREAM CHEESE

Salsa can be purchased ready-made in the refrigerated section of your grocery store, but there are so many degrees of "heat" that many people prefer making their own. Included are two basic recipes you can adjust to your taste. Salsa improves with age, so it's perfect to prepare and store in the refrigerator for up to a week.

8 oz. cream cheese, softened
$1/4$-$1/2$ cup salsa, depending on taste and desired spiciness

Combine ingredients. Makes 6 to 8 servings.

FIESTA SALSA
2 medium tomatoes, mashed or pureed
2 medium avocados, mashed or pureed
1 can (4 oz.) chopped green chilies, drained
$1/4$ cup lemon juice
1 tsp. vegetable oil
1 tsp. sugar
$1/2$ tsp. salt

Combine ingredients. Cover and refrigerate for several hours to blend flavors. Mix desired amount with cream cheese to create bagel spread. Makes 10 to 14 servings.

MEXICAN SALSA

1 can (8 oz.) tomato sauce
2 tbs. red pepper flakes
½ tsp. ground cumin
½ tsp. dried oregano
1 tsp. salt
2 cloves garlic, minced, or ½ tsp. garlic powder
2 tsp. vinegar
juice of ½ lemon

Combine all ingredients. Let stand for 3 hours. Mix desired amount with cream cheese to create bagel spread. Yields about 1¼ cups, or 10 to 12 servings.

JALAPEÑO PEPPER SPREAD

There are mild and hot jalapeño peppers.

8 oz. cream cheese, softened
5 tsp. milk (or enough for spreading consistency)
1/4-1/2 cup finely chopped canned jalapeño peppers, or 1/4 cup finely chopped,
  seeded, fresh jalapeño peppers

Combine ingredients, adding jalapeños according to taste. Makes 6 to 8 servings.

OLD WORLD SPREAD

Serve at room temperature, or pop in the microwave on HIGH for 1 minute and serve warm.

8 oz. cream cheese, softened
1/2 cup margarine, softened
1/4 cup grated Parmesan cheese
2 tbs. dry white wine

2 tbs. chopped fresh parsley
dash pepper
dash dried thyme
dash garlic powder

Combine cream cheese and margarine. Add remaining ingredients and mix well. Makes 8 to 12 servings.

CRUNCHY CUCUMBER SPREAD

*Serve as a bagel spread or as a dip with **Oven-Baked Bagel Chips,** page 160.*

8 oz. cream cheese, softened
½ cup sour cream
1 tbs. milk

1 tsp. grated onion
¼ tsp. Worcestershire sauce
⅓ cup finely chopped cucumber

Combine all ingredients except cucumber, mixing until well blended. Stir in cucumbers. Chill for several hours. Makes 10 to 12 servings.

DILL WITH CREAM CHEESE

This makes a wonderfully different taste for something so easy to make.

8 oz. cream cheese, softened
5 tsp. milk (or enough for spreading consistency)
⅓ cup chopped fresh dill, about 20 sprigs
1 tsp. Dijon mustard

Combine ingredients. Makes 6 to 8 servings.

CHIVES WITH CREAM CHEESE

Top with a slice of onion, or enjoy it just as is.

8 oz. cream cheese, softened
5 tsp. milk (or enough for spreading consistency)
1/4 cup finely chopped fresh chives

Combine ingredients. Makes 4 to 6 servings.

VEGETABLE SPREAD

The vegetables add lots of nutrition as well as crunch.

8 oz. cream cheese, softened
5 tsp. milk (or enough for spreading consistency)
1/3 cup chopped fresh vegetables, any combination: celery, peas, corn, broccoli,
  green bell pepper, cucumber, tomato

Combine ingredients. Makes 10 to 12 servings.

CHEDDAR SPREAD

Here's a spread that's ideal for lunch, buffet supper or an after-theater snack.

8 oz. cream cheese, softened
1 lb. cheddar cheese, shredded
1 tsp. horseradish

1 tsp. Worcestershire sauce
2 oz. Madeira wine or preferred wine

With an electric mixer, whip cream cheese until soft and creamy. Add cheddar cheese in small amounts until combined. Add remaining ingredients and blend. Makes 12 to 16 servings.

CREAM CHEESE WITH ALMONDS AND BELL PEPPER

The bell pepper adds color and taste to this popular spread, especially good on vegetable bagels.

8 oz. cream cheese, softened
5 tsp. milk (or enough for spreading consistency)
1/4 cup chopped blanched almonds
1 tbs. fresh chopped green or red bell pepper, or combination

Combine ingredients. Makes 6 to 8 servings.

RICOTTA CHEESE WITH NUTS

Peanut butter and ricotta are also good as a savory spread, with a little minced garlic, onion and oregano.

½ cup crunchy peanut butter
⅝ cup ricotta cheese
1 tsp. honey

½ cup chopped peanuts
¼ tsp. cinnamon
¼ tsp. nutmeg

Beat peanut butter and ricotta cheese together until fluffy. Stir in honey, nuts and spices. Makes 6 to 8 servings.

GARLIC-PAPRIKA CHEESE SPREAD

Easy, easy, easy and oh, so good!

8 oz. cream cheese, softened
¼ cup mayonnaise

¼ tsp. garlic powder
¼ tsp. paprika

Combine ingredients. Makes 6 to 8 servings.

HEALTHY PEANUT BUTTER SPREAD

Here's a take-off on a Middle Eastern dish that will earn rave notices. Sesame butter, also called tahini, is available in the ethnic section of large grocery stores, or in health food stores.

½ cup toasted soy granules
½ cup peanut butter, chunky or smooth
½ cup sesame butter (tahini)

water as needed
¼ tsp. onion powder
⅛ tsp. garlic powder

Blend soy granules, peanut butter and sesame butter with a fork, a wire whip or a blender. Add water if necessary to attain spreading consistency. Season with onion and garlic powder. Yields 2 cups, or 10 to 14 servings.

APPLE-DATE SPREAD

This one's richly different, and especially suited to health food lovers.

1 apple, cored and quartered
½ cup apple juice

10 pitted dates, chopped
½ cup sunflower seeds

Blend ingredients with a blender or food processor until mixture is of spreading consistency. Yields about 1 cup, or enough for 6 to 8 servings.

GUACAMOLE

Guacamole is normally thought of as a spread or dip that accompanies tortilla chips, cocktail bread or crackers. But it's an excellent spread for bagels, too. Some say that if you place the avocado pit in the mixture until ready to serve, it will help prevent the guacamole from turning dark — others say this is a myth. Making guacamole with a blender will produce a smoother guacamole, easier to spread on a hard bagel.

1 large ripe avocado
1½ tsp. lime juice
¼ tsp. garlic salt
1 tsp. grated onion
1 medium tomato, chopped
1 tbs. mayonnaise

In a medium bowl, mash avocado with a fork. Blend in lime juice and garlic salt. Add remaining ingredients and blend with a fork or, for a smoother result, with a blender. Cover with plastic wrap. Makes 6 to 8 servings.

HUMMUS

Serve this version of a Middle Eastern favorite as a dip or spread.

2 cans (15 oz. each) garbanzo beans
1/3-1/2 cup lemon juice
4 tsp. olive oil

2 cloves garlic, crushed
1/4 cup chopped fresh parsley
1/2 tsp. paprika

Drain garbanzo beans, but retain 1/2 cup liquid and set aside with 1/4 cup beans. In a blender or food processor bowl, puree remaining garbanzo beans with lemon juice. Add about 1/4 cup liquid; add additional liquid slowly as necessary to attain spreading consistency. Stir in oil, garlic, parsley and retained whole beans. Refrigerate for 2 hours to blend flavors. Sprinkle with paprika before serving. Yields 4 cups, or 10 to 14 servings.

EGG AND WALNUT SPREAD

The nuts add crunch and the mustard adds a delightful bite to ordinary egg salad.

4 hard-cooked eggs
1/4 cup chopped walnuts

mayonnaise or light sour cream
1/4 tsp. Dijon mustard, or to taste

Chop eggs in a food processor or force through a sieve. Add enough mayonnaise or sour cream to blend ingredients and achieve a spreading consistency. Add mustard to taste. Spread on bagels or bagel chips. Makes 4 to 6 servings.

CRANBERRY-APPLE SPREAD

This cranberry-based fruit spread is tangy and delicious on bagels.

1 cup sugar
1 cup water
1 pkg. (12 oz.) fresh cranberries
1 apple, cored and finely chopped
1 tsp. cinnamon
1 tsp. nutmeg

In a medium saucepan, boil sugar and water together for 5 minutes. Add cranberries and boil gently without stirring for about 3 minutes. Add apple pieces. Continue boiling until all cranberry skins pop open. Add cinnamon and nutmeg. Remove from heat and cool in saucepan. Transfer to a bowl. Yields 3 cups, or 12 to 16 servings.

CRANBERRY-ORANGE SPREAD

Good whenever fresh cranberries are in season.

1 cup sugar
½ cup water
1 pkg. (12 oz.) fresh cranberries
½ cup orange juice
1 orange, peeled and cut into bite-sized pieces
½-inch square orange peel, finely diced

Boil sugar and water together for 5 minutes. Add cranberries and boil gently without stirring, about 3 minutes. Add orange juice, orange pieces and orange peel pieces. Continue boiling until all cranberry skins pop open. Remove from heat and cool in the saucepan. Yields 3 cups, or 12 to 16 servings.

BAGELWICHES AND BAGEL APPETIZERS

A "bagelwich" is another word for a sandwich. Some bagel restaurants call the food a "sandwich" if the layers are stacked, and a "bagelwich" if it's open-faced. Bagelwiches are often glorified with ingredients piled high and placed under a broiler, if appropriate.

It seems easier to get one's mouth around a bagel sandwich consisting of a softer egg bagel, rather than the traditional water bagel, which has very little "give" to accommodate its ingredients. Soft fillings, such as chopped liver, egg salad and tuna salad, are better on soft bagels. A Reuben sandwich on a hard bagel is better served open-faced. In Miami, Florida, the "scooped" bagel is popular. The bagel is sliced, the center is scooped out and the crust is filled with soft sandwich ingredients.

Small bagels, about 2 inches in diameter, make excellent finger food. Toppings may be cold or broiled for hot hors d'oeuvres. Make bagel canapés with a spread, or try bagel chips with a dip. Serve them with cocktails as hors d'oeuvres or for buffet breakfasts and brunches.

LOX AND CREAM CHEESE ON A BAGEL

This combination has become so well known that some people think it's all one word: "bagels'n'lox" or "lox'n'bagels." Either way, it's become a traditional brunch item in homes across the country, especially on Sunday mornings.

Traditionally, cream cheese is slathered on the bagel and topped with thin, folded slices of lox. That's followed with a slice of tomato and a few sliced onion rounds. It's eaten either as a sandwich or open-faced. Lox is smoked salmon and may be purchased in most delis where bagels are sold. Swedish gravlak may be substituted. It is sweeter than the smoked lox and easy to make at home. Recipes for both follow.

2 oz. cream cheese, softened
1 bagel, sliced in half horizontally
4-6 thin slices lox

2 slices tomato
3-4 slices red or white onion

Spread cream cheese on bagel bottom and cover with slices of lox, tomato and onion; cover with bagel top. Or spread ingredients on each bagel half and eat open-faced.

LOX

While most people find it easier to purchase lox, it can be cured at home easily.

3 lb. center-cut fresh salmon, halved lengthwise,
  backbone and small bones removed
lemon wedges for garnish

LOX MARINADE
¾ cup kosher or coarse salt
6 tbs. brown sugar
1½ tsp. ground white pepper

Scale salmon and pat dry. Rub with mixture of salt, sugar and pepper. Place half of fish, skin side down, in a large casserole that will hold it flat. Rub second half of salmon with marinade and place it, skin side up, on top of bottom piece, with thick end resting over thin end of bottom piece. Cover with foil. Weight down with a large plate or board. Refrigerate for 48 to 72 hours, turning salmon over each day so it cures evenly. Baste with liquid that has accumulated and weight it down again. To serve lox, after removing salmon from marinade, rinse off salt with fresh water and soak in fresh water for about 15 minutes. Slice diagonally. Garnish with lemon wedges. To store, wrap tightly and refrigerate; it will stay tasty and fresh for 3 to 5 days.

SWEDISH GRAVLAK

This popular version of cured salmon is marinated and flavored with dill.

3 lb. center-cut fresh salmon, halved lengthwise,
  backbone and small bones removed
lemon wedges and fresh dill for garnish

SWEDISH GRAVLAK MARINADE

2 tsp. corn oil
4 tbs. coarse salt
4 tbs. sugar

2 tsp. peppercorns, crushed, or 1½ tsp.
  ground white pepper
1 bunch fresh dill, with stalks and crowns

Scale salmon and pat dry. Moisten with oil and rub with mixture of salt, sugar and pepper. Place half of fish, skin side down, in a large casserole that will hold it flat. Cover with a generous layer of dill. Rub second half of salmon with marinade and place it, skin side up, on top of bottom piece with thick end resting over thin end of bottom piece. Add more dill on top and around sides. Cover with foil. Weight down with a large plate or board. Refrigerate for 48 to 72 hours, turning salmon over each day so it cures evenly. Baste with liquid that has accumulated and weight it down again. To serve gravlak, scrape off dill and seasoning and slice diagonally. Garnish with lemon wedges and sprigs of fresh dill. It will keep in the refrigerator, tightly wrapped, for 3 to 5 days.

BAGEL DOG

These are so popular, they're even showing up at airport lunch counters.

1 bagel
large frankfurter or other sausage —
  knockwurst, turkey or chicken franks

mustard, ketchup, relish, barbecue
  sauce or sauerkraut, optional
cheese, sliced or grated, optional

Slice bagel horizontally and toast it if you like. Cut frankfurter into two pieces, and then slice and open each half down the middle lengthwise. Serve one split frankfurter half on top of each bagel half. Add mustard and any other condiments you like, such as ketchup, relish, barbecue sauce or sauerkraut. Add a slice of cheese, or grated cheese, for an extra-good taste. Serve open-faced.

CHEESE AND BACON MELT

This is a wonderful quick lunch when the children rush in from school.

mayonnaise or Thousand Island dressing
1 bagel, split horizontally
3-4 slices bacon, cooked, crumbled, or
  ¼ cup bacon bits

3-6 slices American, Swiss or other
  cheese

Spread dressing on bagel, add bacon and top with cheese. Place under the broiler until cheese melts. Serve open-faced.

BAGEL JALAPEÑO CHEESE-BACON MELT

*For a double whammy, serve this on a **Jalapeño Bagel**, page 81.*

1 slice jalapeño cheese or other cheese   1 tbs. chopped cooked bacon
1 bagel, whole

Lay 1 slice cheese on top of bagel, sprinkle with bacon pieces and heat in the oven, toaster oven or microwave until cheese melts.

CHOPPED CHICKEN LIVER BAGELWICH

Serve with pickles and/or pickled tomatoes as a garnish or side dish. I've included the chicken fat, because it is traditional, but it isn't used much anymore.

1 lb. chicken livers
2 hard-cooked eggs, peeled and
  quartered
1 tsp. grated onion

salt and pepper to taste
¼ cup vegetable oil or melted chicken fat
4-6 bagels, sliced in half horizontally

Broil or bake livers. Chop finely with a food processor or by hand. Add eggs and onion and continue chopping. Add salt, pepper and oil or fat. Blend until mixture is of spreading consistency. Mound liver spread high on each half bagel.

CHICKEN SALAD FOR BAGELS

Always good on a lettuce leaf, this salad is especially good on bagels. Keep the calories at a reasonable level with light mayo and nonfat yogurt, if you like.

2½ cups diced cooked chicken
½ cup finely sliced celery
⅛ cup finely chopped onion
⅓ cup plain yogurt, or as needed

⅓ cup mayonnaise, or as needed
⅛ tsp. curry powder, or to taste
⅛ tsp. pepper, or to taste
4-6 bagels, sliced in half horizontally

Mix chicken, celery and onion together. Add yogurt and mayonnaise in equal amounts as needed until ingredients hold together. Add curry powder and pepper to taste. Mound chicken salad high on each bagel half. Makes 4 to 6 servings.

VARIATIONS
Add ⅓ to ¾ cup of any one or two of the following:
- sliced apples
- halved canned green grapes
- pineapple wedges

- chopped walnuts
- dark or golden raisins

N.Y. REUBEN BAGELWICH

Here's a bagel version of the favorite corned beef sandwich. Serve on a pumpernickel, whole wheat or rye bagel.

1 bagel, sliced
1/4 lb. cooked corned beef, thinly sliced
cole slaw or sauerkraut, drained

2 slices Swiss cheese
4 tomato slices
Russian dressing

Pile bagel halves with corned beef and add cole slaw or sauerkraut, cheese, tomatoes and dressing. Serve cold, or warm in a microwave for about 45 seconds on HIGH or until cheese melts. Serve open-faced.

OMELEGGEL

Try an omelet on a bagel. Slice cooked egg in half to serve open-faced.

2 eggs, beaten
1 tsp. milk, optional
salt and pepper

1 slice American cheese
1 bagel, sliced horizontally

Beat eggs with fork or whisk. Add milk; salt and pepper to taste. Fry in a small pan and keep eggs in a circle the size of a bagel. (Use an egg ring or an egg coral.) Add cheese to omelet when it is partially cooked. Turn eggs over once. Serve on bagel.

MICROWEGGEL

Spray a round china ramekin, about size of bagel, with nonstick vegetable spray. Break 2 eggs into ramekin. Poke egg yolks with a fork tine or tip of a knife. Cover ramekin with plastic wrap. Microwave on HIGH for about 45 seconds to 1 minute or until egg is done to taste. Serve on, or with, a bagel. Divide to serve open-faced.

BAGEL RAREBIT WITH BEER

This is usually made with an egg, but because eating partially cooked eggs is not recommended by health authorities, I have simply deleted it.

1 lb. aged cheddar cheese
1 tbs. butter or margarine
1 cup beer
1 tsp. salt
1 tsp. Worcestershire sauce
½ tsp. paprika

dash cayenne pepper
¼ tsp. curry powder
¼ tsp. dried mustard
8 slices tomato
4 bagels, sliced horizontally and lightly
  toasted

Grate or grind cheese and add butter. Partially melt cheese in a microwave on MEDIUM, stirring frequently; stir in beer. Continue to heat and stir until cheese is melted and beer is warm. Add seasonings and stir. Place a tomato slice on each bagel half and pour rarebit over tomato-topped bagels while hot. Yields 8 servings.

MUENSTER, TOMATO AND SPROUT MELT

These ingredients made a good combination for a bagelwich.

mayonnaise
lettuce
4 slices tomato

alfalfa sprouts
1 bagel, sliced horizontally
4 slices Muenster cheese

Place mayonnaise, lettuce, tomato and sprouts on each bagel half. Top with Muenster cheese. Broil or heat in a microwave on HIGH for about 45 seconds, or until cheese begins to melt.

SLICED SALMON CANAPÉS

These canapés may be served hot or cold.

4 oz. *Chives with Cream Cheese*, page 138
6 mini bagels, sliced in half horizontally
4-6 thin slices lox or gravlak, cut into strips about ¼-inch wide x 2 inches long
sprigs of dill, or 4 tsp. chopped fresh parsley for garnish

Spread cheese mixture thickly on bagels. Lay 3 pieces of salmon crossed over each other on top of cheese. Broil for about 2 minutes or until heated through. Add a sprig of dill on top or sprinkle with parsley.

SMOKED SALMON MOUSSE CANAPÉS

Arrange these pink canapés attractively on a tray and garnish with sprigs of parsley.

8 oz. cream cheese
12 mini bagels, sliced in half horizontally
Smoked Salmon Mousse, page 121, or 8 oz. commercially prepared smoked
   salmon mousse
1 hard-cooked egg, grated
paprika

Spread cream cheese thinly on bagels. Cover with a thin layer of *Smoked Salmon Mousse*. Sprinkle with grated egg and paprika. Makes 24 canapés.

SMOKED SALMON AND LEEK ROULADE CANAPÉS

Salmon rolled around leeks and dill, the diameter of a mini bagel, is sliced and placed on bagel halves to make tasty, attractive canapés. You'll need plastic wrap and two 10-inch lengths of twine.

1 tsp. butter
1 leek, white part only, rinsed clean and cut into long strips
salt
pepper
4 lb. smoked salmon or gravlak, thinly sliced
1 bunch fresh dill
4 oz. cream cheese
1 tsp. Dijon mustard
whipping cream
12 mini pumpernickel bagels, sliced in half horizontally

Melt butter in a sauté pan over medium-high heat and sauté leek strips until just tender. Add salt and pepper to taste. Cool to room temperature.

Lay 1 sheet of plastic wrap (16-x-12 inches) on a smooth work surface. Lay 2 overlapping rows of salmon slices in a large rectangle shape on plastic wrap, leaving 1 inch uncovered around edges. Spread sautéed leek randomly over salmon.

Lift edge of plastic wrap closest to you and carefully roll salmon with leek strips inside into a log shape. (Do not roll the plastic wrap into the log.) Wrap tightly and tie each end securely with twine. Place log in the freezer for several hours or a day to firm.

Break off 25 small sprigs from dill and set aside for a decorative topping. Place remaining sprigs in a food processor with cream cheese and mustard. Process until smooth, or blend with a hand mixer in a mixing bowl. Thin with whipping cream if necessary.

To assemble canapés: Remove salmon log from freezer. Thaw for several hours. Toast bagel halves. Spread dill cream cheese mixture on toasted bagel halves, reserving about 1/4 of the mixture to put in a pastry bag fitted with a Number 2 tip. While salmon is slightly frozen, slice into 24 circles 1/4-inch thick. Place one round on each bagel half. Pipe a dab of remaining dill cream cheese in center of salmon rounds and add 1 dill sprig on top of each. Makes 24 canapés.

OVEN-BAKED BAGEL CHIPS

Slice day-old bagels horizontally into thin slices about ⅛-inch thick. Bake on a greased cookie sheet and place in a preheated 375° oven until browned and crisp, 4 to 5 minutes. Store in an airtight container and serve plain or with dips.

VARIATION: SEASONED BAGEL CHIPS
Brush bagel slices with melted butter or oil and sprinkle with your favorite topping. Try dried herbs, prepared herb or spice blends, paprika, cayenne pepper, sesame seeds, poppy seeds or other favorite seeds, or any of the other suggested toppings listed on pages 27 and 28.

BAGEL BITES

Slice bagels vertically into ⅛-inch slices, so each bite is a small round, and prepare as directed for *Oven-Baked Bagel Chips*.

CHILI-CHEESE BAGEL CHIP NACHOS

Using bagel chips instead of traditional nachos makes this a wonderful variation on the nacho theme and is perfect for appetizers. It's a good way to use up day-old bagels, too.

2 cups chili sauce
1 jar (8 oz.) sharp cheddar cheese spread
8 oz. bagel chips, about 24 chips
1 cup shredded lettuce
1 cup chopped tomato
1/2 cup sour cream

Microwave chili sauce and cheese spread on HIGH for 5 minutes or until thoroughly heated, stirring every 2 minutes. Layer half of chips, half of chili mixture, remaining half of chips and chili mixture on a large platter. Top with shredded lettuce and tomato. Top with sour cream.

BACON-ONION DIP FOR BAGEL CHIPS

If you like dips for bagels or bagel chips, try this delicious one, or add milk to any of the cream cheese spreads to make them of dipping consistency.

8 oz. cream cheese
1/2 cup mayonnaise
4 oz. Swiss cheese, shredded
2 tsp. green onion slices
8 slices bacon, cooked, crumbled
bagel chips

Microwave cream cheese on MEDIUM for 30 seconds or until soft. Mix cream cheese, mayonnaise, Swiss cheese, green onions and crumbled bacon until blended. Spread on bagel chips or use as a dip.

BIBLIOGRAPHY

Bagel, Marilyn and Tom. *The Bagel Bible*. Old Saybrook, CT: Globe Pequot Press, 1992.

Eckhardt, Linda W., and Diana C. Butts. *Bread in Half the Time*. New York, NY: Crown Publishers, 1991.

Fleischmann's Yeast. *Best-Ever Breads*. San Francisco, CA: Burns Philip Food Co., 1993.

German, Donna Rathmell. *The Bread Machine Cookbook*. San Leandro, CA: Bristol Publishing, 1991.

Greenstein, George. *Secrets of a Jewish Baker*. Freedom, CA: Crossing Press, 1993.

Harlow, Jay. *Once Upon A Bagel*. Emeryville, CA: Harlow and Ratner, 1994.

Jones, Judith and Evan. *The Book of Bread*. New York, NY: Harper and Row, 1982.

Lacalamita, Tom. *The Ultimate Bread Machine Book*. New York, NY: Simon and Schuster, 1993.

Langer, Richard W. *The Bread Machine Bakery Book*. New York, NY: Little, Brown, 1991.

Meilach, Dona Z. *Marinades: Make Ordinary Foods Extraordinary*. San Leandro, CA: Bristol Publishing, 1995.

Nathan, Joan. *Jewish Cooking in America*. New York, NY: Alfred A. Knopf, Inc., 1994.

Rehberg, Linda and Lois Conway. *Bread Machine Magic*. New York, NY: St. Martin's Press, 1992.

Ross, Deborah. *The Manischewitz Passover Cookbook*. New York, NY: Walker and Co., 1969.

Zeidler, Judith. *The Gourmet Jewish Cook*. New York, NY: William Morrow, 1988.

BAGEL SUPPLY SOURCES

Need information? Look for telephone numbers listed on packages. Many companies offer information and help. They have booklets, help sheets and catalogs for the asking.

Arrowhead Mills, Inc. - flours, vital gluten
PO Box 2059
Hereford, TX 79045
806 364-0730

The Chef's Catalog - baking equipment, bagel
    slicers, bread makers and mixers
3215 Commercial Ave.
Northbrook, IL 60062
708 480-9400

Fleischmann's Yeast - yeast
PO Box 7004
San Francisco, CA 94108
800 777-4959 - baker's help line

General Mills, Inc.
Box 200-SP
Minneapolis, MN 55440

Gold Medal - hints, information, how to read
    dating codes
800 328-6787

Great Valley Mills - flours, fruit butters, fruit
    spreads
RD 3, County Line Road
Box 1111
Barto, PA 19504
800 688-6455

King Arthur Flour Baker's Catalog - flours,
    baking supplies, dried fruits, seeds, spices
Box 1010
Norwich, VT 05055
800 827-6836

K-TEC - flours, grains, baking supplies, Kitchen
    Champ mixer
420 N. Geneva Rd
Linden, UT 84042
800 288-6455

Mountain Woods, Inc. - fiddle bow bread knives
PO Box 65
East Glacier Park, MT 59434
800 835-0479

Out of the Woods - fiddle bow bread knives
    and bagel cutters
33556 Bloomberg Road
Eugene, OR 97405
800 713-3245

Red Star Yeast - yeast
A Division of Universal Foods Corporation
PO Box 737
Milwaukee, WI 53201
800 445-4746 #4 - baker's help line

SAF-Instant Yeast - yeast
Minneapolis, MN 55415
800 641-4615

Walnut Acres - dried fruits, flours, baking
    supplies
Penns Creek, PA 17862
800 433-3998

Williams-Sonoma - baking supplies, yeasts,
    spread ingredients, machines
PO Box 7456
San Francisco, CA 94120-7456
800 541-2233 - catalog sales
800 541-1262 - customer service

BAGEL MAKING VIDEO TAPE
For a video tape about making bagels with
    different equipment, techniques and
    ingredients,contact:
The Bagel Making Video
2018 Saliente Way - Suite B
Carlsbad, CA 92009

INDEX

SERVE CREATIVE, EASY, NUTRITIOUS MEALS WITH NITTY GRITTY® COOKBOOKS